CW01019333

DAF

DAF

TRUCKS TODAY

Eric Gibbins

MOTOR RACING PUBLICATIONS LTD
28 Devonshire Road, Chiswick, London W4 2HD, England

ISBN 0 900549 60 2
First published 1981

Copyright © 1981 — Eric Gibbins and Motor Racing
Publications Ltd

All rights reserved. No part of this publication may be
reproduced, stored in a retrieval system, or transmitted, in
any form or by any means, electronic, mechanical,
photocopying, recording or otherwise, without the prior
permission of Motor Racing Publications Ltd.

Photosetting by Zee Creative Ltd., London SW16.
Printed in Great Britain by The Garden City Press Limited,
Letchworth, Hertfordshire SG6 1JS.

Contents

About the author

ERIC GIBBINS is one of Britain's most experienced and highly respected commercial-vehicle writers with a journalistic career dating from 1953, when he joined *Motor Transport* as an editorial assistant. He subsequently became assistant editor of that journal before taking over the editorship of the magazine *Commercial Vehicles* in 1962. He left journalism for a short period in order to take up a senior public relations appointment within the industry, but by 1970 he was once again writing full-time, soon to become editor and publisher of the *Freight Industry Yearbook* and *Truck & Bus Builder*. His intimate knowledge of all aspects of the commercial-vehicle industry, and in particular of truck design, construction and operation, has been invaluable in ensuring the accuracy and authority of these one-make histories in the TRUCKS TODAY series.

Introduction

In the context of commercial vehicle production, DAF of Eindhoven counts as the youngest major manufacturer in Europe. As such, the company exhibits many of the characteristics of the youthful executive willing to try new ideas in both the manufacturing and marketing spheres.

This attitude to innovation, however, is tempered with the solid reliability that people associate with the Dutch. This is particularly reflected in the fact that the product is painstakingly designed to fulfil the customer's needs as opposed to what the designer thinks they should be.

In its examination of the truck market, the company's management has been shrewd in putting their emphasis on the heavy vehicle end of the market, where the domestic industry in the Netherlands is particularly strong. This owes a great deal to the country's location in Europe with its main centres of international trade. DAF also realized at an early stage of its development that a strong service and parts network on international routes was the key to success.

These factors, coupled with the attention given to providing products which the customer wanted and their reliability, have provided the cornerstones of success. In attempting to explain DAF's success — in the last decade particularly — it is interesting to see how often these characteristics are to be found.

In preparing the manuscript for this book I particularly wish to acknowledge the help of DAF personnel in both the Netherlands and the UK, notably Mr Dave Mansell, Mr Phil Ives, Mr Chris Thorneycroft-Smith and Mr Hans Meyer, whose help has been greatly valued.

Eric Gibbins

The original — and very basic — workshop of Hub van Doorne at Eindhoven, which was the foundation stone to the build-up of the DAF empire.

In vivid contrast with the original premises, DAF's main office block at Eindhoven, which includes an attractive display of DAF products old and new.

Chapter 1

Founding an empire

As a European truck manufacturer DAF is unique in two ways; it is the only company that has made the big league in heavy truck production starting from scratch after World War 2 and it is the only manufacturer to shift successfully from trailer building into powered vehicle construction. The measure of its success is easy to quantify. In 1979, the company set a manufacturing record for itself by building 15,547 heavy and medium-weight commercial vehicles. Thirty years before that, the company had had prototypes on the road, but it had yet to go into full production with its vehicles.

The early history of DAF has been described many times before, not least by my friend Pat Kennett in his excellent book on DAF in the *World Trucks* publications. In this my second book in the *Trucks Today* series, however, I shall be concentrating on the more recent history; outlining the pattern of development that has led to DAF Trucks as it is at the present time in terms of both its products and as a company. Nevertheless, it would be totally remiss of me not to acknowledge and applaud the work of the men who made it all possible, Hub J. van Doorne and his brother Wim who, rightly, are spoken of not just with respect but also with a touch of reverence by anyone who had the privilege to work with or for them.

Hub van Doorne's history is remarkable in these days of university degrees, doctorates, computers and microchips. He certainly had an unusual beginning for he came into the world

on the first day of the year 1900, and as if that wasn't enough, he managed to be born in America! But America was in Holland in this case, for it was the name of a small village in the province of Limburg.

He had little education, left school at 12 and had a string of jobs in the next 10 years or so from working in a blacksmith's shop to chauffeuring a well-known local doctor, before he established, with his savings, a motorcycle and cycle shop. After two years this 'went bust'. When he was 14 he applied for a job with the Philips electrical company in Eindhoven, but didn't get it because he failed a test on calculating fractions. That was to be one of the best things that ever happened to him; he just might have got the job and stayed there for a long, long time, in which case there would have been no DAF trucks today.

The turning point for him came in the early-1920s, when he was allowed to tinker with the very expensive car of a local brewer and remedied an irritating fault which nobody had been able to correct. The brewer, by the name of Hueges, recognized a hidden talent and he offered to finance him in business. A year later Hub took him up on the offer on the proviso that his young brother, Wim, was also involved. Such, briefly, was the prelude to the formation of Commanditaire Vennootschap Hub van Doorne's Maschinenfabriek — no wonder later they called it DAF — in April 1928. The partnership between the two brothers proved an ideal one, with Hub the engineering genius and Wim the

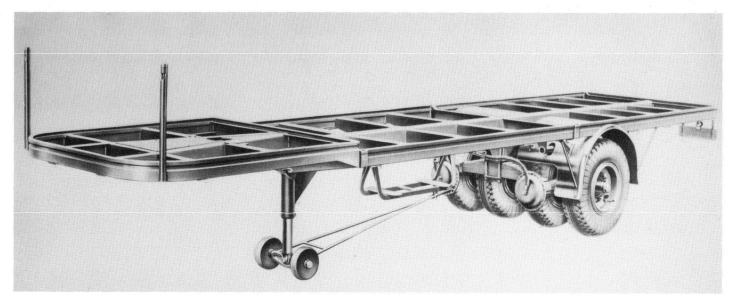

Twin oscillating axles to produce a higher weight capacity were a feature of this early Featherlite trailer design from DAF; it had a herringbone frame structure, which created a sensation at the 1934 Amsterdam Motor Show.

DAF's single-spine Featherlite chassis with twin oscillating axles was used for both semi-trailers and, as in this instance, drawbar trailers.

responsible business sense.

Although both of them were committed to road vehicle development, the difficult economic conditions of the period dictated that they take on general engineering work as well, which they did with no small measure of success. By 1930, the factory had increased in size from 160 m² to 1600 m² and

An interesting feature of DAF's twin-oscillating-axled semi-trailer was that each pair of axles could be turned on its own axis. This simplified maintenance work as each wheel could be worked on with equal facility.

Special semi-trailers, like this display unit built for DAF's Eindhoven neighbour Philips, were just one of DAF's many-sided trailer-making activities.

business was so good, even in this period of world depression, that in 1932 a joint stock company was formed and the name changed to Van Doorne's Aanhangwagenfabriek or, translated, the van Doorne trailer factory — DAF for short.

The 1930s saw a feast of ideas in trailer construction emerging from DAF. One which put the company out in front, and which appeared at the Amsterdam Show in 1934, was the 'featherweight', a semi-trailer which, because of design features, was 40 per cent lighter than conventional designs. Instead of a conventional ladder-frame chassis it consisted of a single, central, box-section girder with a close-pitched cross-member welded to it on each side and reinforced at the running gear's mounting points. The suspension was, perhaps, the most unusual characteristic, comprising two semi-elliptic leaf springs mounted transversely just ahead and to the rear of the twin oscillating axles, each with two wheels, which formed the four-wheels-in-line running unit. A feature of this design was that each axle pivotted on its own axis, so that by turning the axle maintenance work could be done on the inner wheel with equal facility as on the outer.

Two years on there was yet another important innovation as the Daflosser was created. This was a vehicle consisting of a tractor unit and swan-neck, low-loading, very short semi-trailer, fitted with a tilting platform superstructure designed to permit the loading and off-loading of containers on to and from railway wagons.

PHILIPS

Moment for celebration in 1953. The principal of Delft University of Technology awards the self-taught engineer Hub van Doorne with an honorary doctorate.

indications of the engineering ingenuity of Hub van Doorne, but there were plenty more to come as DAF made its first incursion into the world of powered vehicles. This happened in the same year as the Daflosser was produced and it involved the development of an all-wheel-drive vehicle called the Trado. The name derives from the association Hub van Doorne had on this project with a military man named van der Trappen, with the first three letters of the latter being married with the first two of Doorne. This was to be the first stage of a long involvement in military vehicle production for DAF, which has continued through to the present day.

The Trado system could virtually be applied to any civilian vehicle and it was claimed that it could turn one into a 6 × 4 cross-country vehicle in a matter of four hours. The first stage in the conversion was to remove the original wheels and substitute the Trado's two tandem wheels. The normal propeller-shaft was connected to the back axle differential in the usual way, but there convention ended, for each wheel was driven by a short stub-axle connected to the main axle,

These containers were mounted on flat platforms fitted with skate wheels, which recessed into channels fitted transversely on the railway wagons. Chocks prevented their lateral movement in transit, but removal of the chocks permitted them to be pushed manually sideways on to the superstructure of the road vehicle. This consisted of a frame below which was an hydraulic ram. Manipulation of the ram allowed an adjustable extension to the frame, fitted with channels similar to those on the railway wagon, to line-up with the rail wagon's channels for the container to be run on and secured. By extending the ram, the frame was tilted around the pivot point to the rear of the semi-trailer's axle so that the frame extension made contact with the ground and the container could be run off. This was an idea which was adopted by a number of rail transport concerns, not only in the Netherlands, but in Germany, Belgium and Switzerland as well.

Novel trailer designs like these were the first real

Hub van Doorne, studying a drawing of a six-cylinder engine, explains a point to one of his leading engineers in the 1950s.

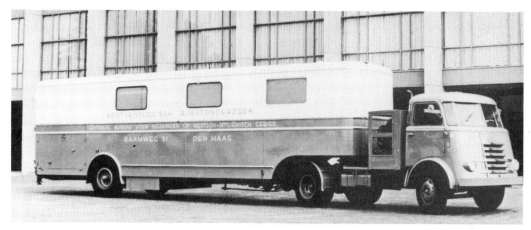

A mobile X-ray unit built in the early-1950s and hauled by a DAF T 1500 R tractor unit. This model was fitted with the Perkins 108 bhp 5.56-litre diesel engine and was built for operation at a gross combination weight of 22 tonnes.

the stub-axles on each side of the vehicle being housed in what has been termed a longitudinal swinging rocker.

DAF's first military vehicle, an armoured car, was subsequently developed using this design and the British Army negotiated a licence to build the vehicle. It was never, in fact, taken up as World War 2 intervened before proper arrangements could be put in hand.

All kinds of strange vehicles emerged from this Trado design, not least one fitted with a disc saw in place of one of the wheels to act as an ice-breaker truck. This, too, was a military vehicle development, for the Dutch Government's defence plan was to flood the country's low-lying areas in the event of invasion; it was a plan which would not work in a hard winter in freezing conditions.

One of the first moves by the Germans after the invasion of the Netherlands in 1940 was, naturally, to take over the DAF factory, which by then was no small enterprise; it employed 280 people and covered an area of 100,000 ft² (9,290 m²). But they received no co-operation from the van Doornes. In fact, the Germans had to put one of their own men in charge and Hub van Doorne cut himself off from involvement by feigning sickness.

The four-year period of occupation of the Netherlands by the Germans was not entirely wasted by Hub and Wim van Doorne for, in this period, they laid down plans for the years

to come after the Germans had been defeated. It was then, in fact, that they designed the vehicles which later were to be produced by DAF as their first proper commercial vehicle range.

When the war ended they were anxious to make a start on powered vehicle production, but the move did not even begin until three years after hostilities had ended, although production of trailers and semi-trailers had been restarted straight away to get transport going again in this war-ravaged country.

The van Doorne brothers, having set their sights on developing powered vehicles, enlisted the help of the Dutch Government with a view to setting-up facilities straight away. Rightly, however, they suddenly realized that the end of the war would bring a flood of war-surplus trucks on to the market, and so the brothers had to back-pedal in spite of having won over the Dutch Government to their way of thinking. In the event it was to be five years after the war that the first powered vehicles were to come off the production line, although prototypes appeared as early as 1948.

One of the natural benefits for DAF as a truck builder was that, although the Dutch market was territorially small, the Dutch haulage industry was inevitably a considerable force in transport, based as it was on the doorstep of Europe. With the development of the Dutch and Belgian ports in the 1950s

and 1960s, particularly Rotterdam as the largest in Europe and Antwerp the second biggest, a tremendous and expanding traffic flow gave the Dutch haulier a natural advantage. The situation created a much higher than normal demand for vehicles, particularly big outfits, not just to cope with fairly local docks traffic but, increasingly, for long hauls to other European countries and, later, the Middle East.

1950 marked the beginning of DAF as it is today, for it was in April of that year that the van Doornes established what was then probably the most advanced, if not very large, truck plant in Europe covering 9,000 m² and employing 184 people. As a measure of its facilities, 746 vehicles were built by the end of 1950, a figure which increased to over 1,000 in the following first full production year — quite a high output at that time for a completely new venture.

Left, the workforce takes a moment off to celebrate the manufacture of the 10,000th DAF truck in 1953. Below and below left, technical innovation was not confined to DAF's truck and trailer activities. These unusual roll-out engines were a feature of bus chassis, and the concept attracted considerable interest when it was exhibited at the 1948 Amsterdam Motor Show. Easy maintenance was the object.

The first vehicles off the line were 5-tonners, designed in the wartime days and developed in prototype form in 1948 and 1949. In fact, the first examples were built at the company's trailer plant while the new factory was still being built.

The 50-series truck, as it was known, had a 4 × 2 configuration and a designed gross weight of 7 tonnes as a load carrier. There was a choice of two engines, a four-cylinder Hercules 4.62-litre petrol engine producing 102 bhp at 3,000 rpm or a Perkins P6-80 4.73-litre diesel rated at 83 bhp at 2,400 rpm. Both were matched with a four-speed heavy-duty gearbox. One model was distinguished from the other by adopting the prefix A for the petrol-engined vehicles and D for the diesels, thus A50-1 was the petrol and D50-1 the diesel.

There was nothing particularly startling about the design; it

Quite a number of DAFs in the 1950s were fitted with custom-built bodies and cabs like this example constructed for furniture carrying.

was very much a bread-and-butter specification except for the fact that it had an electrically-welded pressed-steel frame similar to that used on the famous Featherlight trailers. Otherwise, it had vacuum-hydraulic brakes, a fully-floating hypoid-bevel-gear rear axle, and cam-and-lever-type steering gear. Tyres were 8.25—20, 12-ply on eight-bolt steel disc wheels, twinned on the rear, and the suspension was provided by a normal semi-elliptic spring design. In addition to the load carriers, the 50-series was offered as a tractor for articulated vehicle use at 13 tonnes gross combination weight.

DAF produced its own very distinctive cab design for the 50-series, giving the Dutch company's vehicles a look which was basically not to change too much until well into the 1960s. It was a forward-control design and, as such, seems to have established a permanent pattern for this configuration for DAF vehicles thereafter. There have been some bonneted models, but they have been few in number.

The 50-series was the bedrock of DAF's development as a truck manufacturer. It was not, however, a series on its own. There was a 40-series and a 60-series as well, the former designed for operation at just on 8 tonnes and available with less powerful engines, the Perkins diesel being derated, for example, to 70 bhp, while the output of the Hercules petrol engine was 91 bhp. The 60-series was built for operation at 10.5 tonnes gross weight, but in fact fitted much the same range of engines as the 50-series except that the Hercules diesel was offered in addition to the petrol version and the Perkins diesel. The Hercules diesel had a bigger engine capacity than its petrol counterpart, producing 96 bhp. When fitted in the largest available outfit, it permitted a lorry and drawbar trailer to be rated at 19 tonnes gross train weight.

Taken together, however, and counting the wheelbase permutations available, DAF offered a surprisingly large number of different models in this its first effort. The range was unveiled to the public, predictably at the Amsterdam Show, in 1951.

In the early-1950s, the manufacture of military vehicles was to play a big part in DAF's development and this aspect of the company's activities is so important — for several years in the 1950s manufacture of military vehicles was more than 50 per cent of total production — that it is treated separately in another chapter.

On the commercial vehicle front, it did not take the company long to start extending its products. Special municipal models were built for the first time in 1953 and a bus range was also introduced. A further step was the construction of a 4 × 4 tipper chassis.

Even in this short period of three years, DAF was starting to show that it was likely to become a force to be reckoned with, but that's in hindsight, for few people outside the Netherlands then regarded DAF as anything more than a small domestic producer. There were some in the country who had such faith, however, and certainly Hub van Doorne's talents were particularly recognized. The outward sign of this was the hitherto unheard-of distinction of the Delft University of Technology conferring an honorary doctorate on Hub in recognition of his achievements in the field of engineering.

Delft's Professor Broeze, in conferring the honour, referred to Hub's remarkable background, sadly commenting that the best engineer coming from Delft was one who had achieved this eminence without ever acquiring the basic knowledge which was considered at Delft to be indispensable in the education of an engineer. This was a hard blow to Delft's academic pride. He emphasized that the University of Delft deeply regretted not having had the opportunity to count Mr van Doorne on its students' roll.

The next main stage in development came in 1955, when the range was given a facelift and the 1100, 1300 and 1500 models were introduced with ratings of 8.4, 10.1 and 11 tonnes, respectively, and powered by the Leyland 0.350 engine. Fitment of this power unit formed part of an agreement for DAF to take Leyland engines, the first move towards an agreement for DAF to build Leyland engines under licence.

It was from the Leyland 0.350 engine that DAF derived its own DD 575, which went into production in 1957, but still with many components supplied by Leyland. This was the start by DAF of the manufacture of its own major components. By the 1970s DAF was to build everything that was really important other than clutches and gearboxes. 1958, for instance, saw the start of axle production within the company, and the following year the engine range was

One of the few bonneted models produced by DAF was the Series 16 DD. Introduced in 1959 as part of the 1500 and 1600 series, it was fitted with a DAF DD 575 engine producing 120 bhp at 2,400 rpm.

extended with the introduction of the DA 475 and the DS 575. These engines were to mark a move by DAF up the chassis weight scale to the 1600 and 1800-series, the 1600, built for operation at 12 tonnes gross weight, replacing the 1500-series, and the 1800-series coming in at 14 tonnes gross and fitting the DS575.

In pursuing the engine theme, however, an important chassis development has been ignored. It is important not because it is in any way particularly significant, but because it was unusual for DAF. The company introduced a bonneted range — only two such ranges were ever produced, apart from 'specials', and this was the first. The 13 and 15-series, as

the vehicles were called, featured 83 bhp or 115 bhp petrol engines. The 13-series was built to operate at 13 to 22 tonnes gcw as a tractor unit or 9.5 tonnes as a solo vehicle. The 15-series operated in the same gross combination weight bracket as an artic tractor unit, but at 11 tonnes gross as a solo load carrier. Leyland and Perkins diesels were the options as power units in both these models.

It was, however, the 1500, 1600 and 1800-series which took DAF into the 1960s, and it was very largely to be vehicle weights and dimensions legislation which was to influence the development of many of the models produced from this point on.

The best sellers in the 1950s — the 50-series

Type:	A 50-1 and D 50-1, payload 6.6 tonnes, gross weight 9.2 tonnes; 16 tonnes gtw when hauling drawbar trailer.
Engine:	In A 50-1, Hercules, 4.62-litre, six-cylinder, side-valve petrol engine, producing a maximum power output of 102 bhp @ 3,200 rpm and a maximum torque of 187 lb ft @ 1,400 rpm. In D 50-1, Perkins 4.73-litre, six-cylinder P6 in-line diesel engine producing a maximum power output of 83 bhp @ 2,400 rpm and a maximum torque of 187 lb ft @ 1,400 rpm.
Gearbox:	Four-forward-speed constant-mesh unit with five-speed constant-mesh unit and two-speed rear axle as options.
Overall length:	6.35 m.
Wheelbase:	3.9 m.
Front axle:	I-beam, capacity 3.5 tonnes.
Rear axle:	Fully floating, hypoid-bevel gear, capacity 5.3 tonnes, ratio 5.84:1 or, optionally, 6.8:1.
Steering gear:	Cam-and-lever.
Brakes:	Hydraulic with vacuum booster.
Suspension:	Semi-elliptic springs, suspended in rubber without shackles, and double-acting telescopic shock absorbers on front axle.

Above left, DAF's 40, 50 and 60 series were the bedrock of its design programme in the 1950s. This photograph shows a 5-tonner from this family at work on snow-plough duties. Left, a typically Dutch setting for this 50-series vehicle shown here as a lorry-and-trailer outfit which could operate at 17 tonnes gross.

Chapter 2

Company development

One of the charactertistics of DAF in the 1950s and 1960s which made it stand out from other European manufacturers was that it retained a family atmosphere. This, of course, centred on the van Doorne family through the active working roles of the brothers Hub and Wim. Inevitably, as the company expanded, this lessened, but even in the 1980s it is still there to some degree.

The second generation of the van Doornes is as active as the first, albeit in a different working and trading environment, with Mr Piet van Doorne, son of Hub, as president and chairman of the Board of Management, with his brother, Martin, as president of the Supervisory Board and Mr Willie van Doorne, son of Wim, as managing director of the European Domestic Division.

Something of DAF's philosophy came through when the company celebrated its golden jubilee in 1978 and Mr Piet van Doorne spoke at the Paris Motor Show to let people know DAF's views on a variety of topics; not least he presented a self-scrutiny of the company and the path opening up for it in the future. As his comments gave a good insight into DAF on the threshold of the 1980s, it is worth quoting what he had to say at some length.

He started off by referring to the real start of the company's operations with the first trickle of trucks from the production line in 1949. Since then, he said, the company had taken a step forward virtually every year, with regular increases in the number of products and of components for products developed and put into production.

He went on to say: 'We believe that DAF's growth has always been based on the good quality and original technical features of its products. Another pillar on which the company rests is the quality of the organization which markets and maintains these products. This organization does honour to the name of DAF Trucks and strengthens its reputation in transport circles. These pillars have always proved a firm basis, enabling us to keep going and remain in a sound position even in difficult times.'

He talked about the then current forecasts of other leading European commercial vehicle manufacturers, who foresaw difficult times ahead and threw doubt upon the chances of survival of the smaller manufacturers. Their arguments, he commented, were based on the fact that the European market was not showing any more growth and had become a buyer's market in which supply exceeded demand. 'My answer is that throughout the entire history of our company, we have acted as if we were faced with a buyer's market,' adding that, 'this means that we meet customers' wishes wherever possible and build up a relationship with them that continues after the purchase has been made.'

He was aware, he said, that this approach was often no longer feasible in very large companies. That was why DAF attached much importance to the expression 'small is beautiful' since it was felt that it applied to DAF. It might, he pointed out, be the reason why the company had to date

An early-1950s picture of the production line at the Eindhoven factory showing the method of cab construction then employed.

expanded more rapidly than most of its competitors. Starting from scratch, and working in conditions that had not always been favourable, the company had reached its present position in the commercial vehicle field in the comparatively short period of 30 years.

Mr van Doorne went on to say: 'Five years ago we wrote in our financial annual report that a clear trend towards greater cost-consciousness could be perceived in the Western European transport world. Attention was increasingly being focussed on product reliability, service quality and driver comfort. Looking at our growth figures, with production rising from 9,400 in 1973 to 13,000 in 1977, you may agree with me that this trend has not been a problem to us and that our buyers' market way of thinking has been the right one.'

He then turned his attention to the then current position and the future. Earlier in the year, DAF had produced its new long-term plan and marked out the course for the coming years. To ensure DAF's future as an independent company, it had opted for a selective growth strategy in which efforts would be devoted mainly to the products and markets with, and in which, the company had already reached a certain level, and which were susceptible to further improvement. This implied concentration on the strong areas. The company's general competitiveness, as built up in the past, provided a good starting point for such growth. He pointed out that DAF was soundly established in its own Benelux home market, but would have to strengthen its position in other European markets. It was also important that the company's position in non-European markets be maintained and, where possible, improved. In some of those markets, local assembly would involve increasing commercial vehicle production to at least 16,000 units in 1982, with the emphasis on medium-heavy and heavy vehicles.

To achieve the necessary growth, it was essential that the sales network be strengthened. Besides being expanded geographically, it would be upgraded and would provide better coverage. To promote exports to overseas markets, such as those in the Middle East and Africa, a range of products derived from the present heavy and medium-heavy ranges would be developed specially for these markets in the next few years.

Nothing has really changed for DAF since Mr van Doorne made these comments except that production went up to close on 15,000 vehicles in 1979. But what was the build-up in company terms, which resulted in the remarks being made at all?

Back in the early-1950s expansion was rapid. The 9,000 m² vehicle factory (which came to be known as DAF 1) which opened in April 1950 had become too small for the company in a matter of two years. Therefore, a second factory was built, to be termed the DAF 2 plant, and this opened in May 1953, the year when DAF celebrated its 25th anniversary. Some idea of the extent of the company's early expansion can be gauged from the fact that in 1950 the work force was 184 and in 1953, when the new factory opened, it had jumped to 1,100 and to 1,700 in the total organization.

The expansion continued, 1955 seeing the company build its 10,000th truck and 1957 the start of engine, axle and cab manufacture, the engine being the Leyland 0.350 power unit made under licence.

It was in the following year that the van Doornes embarked on their diversification into car manufacture, a development that obviously was to have a big impact on commercial vehicle production.

The initial success with the car, known originally as the DAF 600, is now almost folklore. Even though it was not in production when unveiled to the public, orders for over 4,000 from the Netherlands alone were taken at its launch at the Amsterdam Motor Show of 1958 and, when dealers were sought, DAF had over 1,400 applications. The vehicle featured, of course, the Variomatic belt-driven transmission which had no gearbox and no differential and was driven by a tiny 600 cc two-stroke air-cooled engine.

A maximum production figure of 100 per day had been envisaged, but this had to be revised upwards because of the interest created. A programme to get production started was put in hand straight away, but the production line was not finished until the spring of 1959, and just 700 cars were to be built by the end of the year, although around 30,000 were to be built in the next two years and total production had reached 100,000 by 1964. There was a substantial investment in the car programme and the design had its share of teething troubles in its early days.

It is difficult, even at this point in time, to say whether the car venture was a good or bad thing for DAF for it must have slowed commercial vehicle development and soaked up

Eindhoven is the location for DAF engine development and manufacture. This is the end of the production line with trolley-mounted power units awaiting installation in chassis.

21

capital. Not that it appeared to at first, for in 1962 DAF doubled its trailer production by increasing the capacity of its trailer plant through the construction of a new factory at Geldrop. One benefit of the car programme, of course, was that there were a whole host of commercial vehicle developments (see the next two chapters) which made use of components developed for the car.

On the truck side, 1958 was also a landmark for DAF for it was in that year that annual commercial vehicle production exceeded that for military use. Moreover, as indicated earlier, it was also the first year of manufacture of key components, with the quality control benefits which that implied.

Construction of DAF's 50,000th commercial vehicle was celebrated in July 1964, and annual production was steadily rising — by 1969 it had risen to 6,770 to reach a grand total of 76,000 from the start of manufacture. By this time DAF had over 40 per cent of the home market in the Netherlands and employed 10,000 people (including those engaged in car production and sales).

In the mid-1960s, however, there were production capacity problems, and car manufacturing requirements were having an impact on the commercial vehicle output. At this time, DAF had many Belgian workers crossing the frontier daily to work at the company's plants. For that, and local labour

The F 200 tilt cab on the F 700/900 series was developed as part of the Club of Four project. This one dates from 1974.

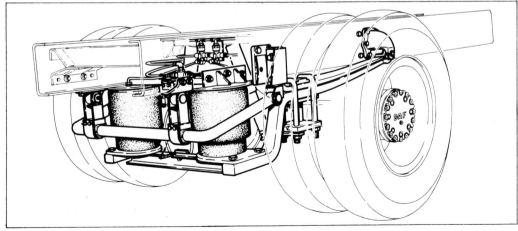

DAF's air suspension, shown here on the rear axle of a vehicle of the mid-1970s, was attached to the chassis frame with two special two-leaf guide springs, mounted on pivots at the front in the original spring brackets. The other ends are shaped to fit in guide plates on the chassis frame to give sideways location to the axle. The lower spring leaves continue downwards and are linked by a crossbeam immediately behind the axle. The two air bellows are mounted on this beam. Air for the suspension system comes from a separate air reservoir, so that it is independent of the braking system.

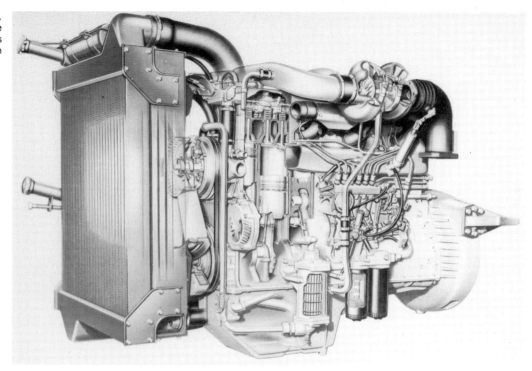

DAF's six-cylinder, turbocharged, charge-cooled DKS 1160 E diesel engine was developed as part of the company's plan to secure greater fuel efficiency in the vehicles it offered.

shortage reasons, it was decided to build a plant at Oeval, just over the Belgian side of the Dutch-Belgian frontier, for cab construction and axle manufacture. This happened in 1966 and expansion there has been such that this plant covers an area of 53,000 m² in the 1980s.

With cab production divorced from Eindhoven, space was left for car engine production, but there was still not enough room for the rapidly expanding car production needs. Moreover, there was a labour shortage at Eindhoven, and this led to an important development for DAF. It was decided that a totally new car production plant should be built, but not at Eindhoven.

There was a recession in the Dutch coal mining industry at this time in the area around Limburg, which had consequently become an area of high unemployment. Talks

with the Dutch Ministry of Economic Affairs and the Dutch State Mines resulted in a decision to build a car plant in this area — at Born, near Sittard.

DAF moved fast, and in less than 12 months after the decision, the first car was built at the new factory, which covered an area of 70,000 m² and, three months later, the last one was built at Eindhoven.

This development was of real significance in the history of the company because, as part of the fund-raising deal by which the Born operation was mounted, and since national interests were involved, the Dutch State Mines acquired a 25 per cent interest in the company.

Until the Born factory was built, car production was concentrated on the DAF 44, a more modern looking and more powerful development of the original design, which derivatives of these little passenger cars, the DAF 33, for example, also being produced as a van or a pick-up, while the 44, 55 and 66 were all available in station wagon guise.

At Eindhoven, meanwhile, work was progressing on DAF's engine development programme, 1968 seeing the introduction of the 11.6-litre DAF diesel and the phasing out of engines built by other manufacturers. Every company has its lean times as well as its good ones, and the early-1970s proved difficult for DAF. It was then that the company felt the need for resources greater than its own, and in 1972 DAF signed a co-operation agreement with International Harvester.

The reasoning behind this was well explained by Mr Piet van Doorne in 1978, when it was rumoured that IH might

What is a picture of a boxer doing here? As part of its promotion programme DAF Trucks sponsors various sporting events, including the Middleweight Championship of the World. This is Alan Minter, who defended his title first (successfully) against Vito Antuofermo and in September 1980 (unsuccessfully) against Marvin Hagler.

itself had grown into the DAF 750, then the Daffodil and more recently the DAF 33. But within months of Born coming on stream another new model, the Renault-engined DAF 55, was to appear which, in turn, would be developed in time into the DAF 66. There were various commercial

DAF sponsors cycling in the Netherlands and in particular it has an interest in a Dutch team which races throughout Europe. This is their badge.

take over DAF completely. What he said on that occasion effectively killed the rumours.

When DAF signed the co-operation agreement with IH there were, he said, three basic considerations. First, strengthening of DAF's finances to allow for growth; secondly, creation of possibilities of selling DAF products in other markets, including North America (it was also anticipated that IH would market certain models from its own vehicle range in Europe through DAF's sales channels); thirdly, wherever possible the two companies would make use of each other's know-how and engineering and development facilities.

He then explained what had happened since then. The capital injection stemming from IH's purchase of 33 per cent of the DAF equity had had exactly the effect planned and had made it possible for DAF to grow to the size it was in 1978. However, because of the drop in the exchange rate of the US dollar in relation to the Dutch guilder since 1972, DAF products had become too expensive for the North American market, so IH had not taken advantage of that part of the agreement.

He went on to develop this point, saying: 'European views about the technical concept of a truck differ from those of our US partner because, among other things, the market requirements are not the same. Another important factor is that the two companies each have their own attitudes and

Care was taken in 1969, when this six-wheeler-and-trailer outfit was being tested, that no-one should know that it was a new design. It was fitted with a prototype F 218 tilt cab, which was to be announced in 1970 on the 2000 series.

A 2800-series lorry and drawbar trailer seen on test in the late-1970s to evaluate the performance of the DKS 1160 E 'economy' engine.

ways of working which are difficult to keep in line.'

These, said Mr van Doorne, were the reasons why the present co-operation between DAF Trucks and IH had to be regarded purely as financial. He questioned: 'You might wonder whether DAF Trucks will be able to finance its ambitious long-term plans without outside assistance. Well, the answer is "Yes".'

In the last few years, investment in DAF Trucks had, he said, been high enough for the present technical capacity for truck production to be put at more than 18,000 a year. In the case of some components, including engines, the capacity was

much higher. The planned increase in production did not, therefore, call for further major investment.

DAF believed — again on the strength of the careful analysis on which the company's long-term plan was based — that it would be capable of self-financing in the next few years all other investment which might be needed for expansion of the sales organization and for improvements to, and renewal of, the DAF product range.

These comments by Mr van Doorne explained a lot, for the IH deal meant that DAF had had finance for expansion in the 1970s when it needed it, and it is not without significance that

As with all modern heavy vehicle manufacturers, DAF has a very extensive vehicle development programme, which includes off-road testing (as with this FAD 2205 DU 8 × 4 tipper chassis, right, equipped with test weights), road testing (as with the F700/F900, below, negotiating a tight corner) and manoeuvrability and suspension testing (as with this 2000-series 6 × 2 vehicle, below right, loaded with test weights).

One of the few outward signs of DAF's link with International Harvester was this International with special cab and DAF semi-trailer sold through the Dutch company.

some of its most successful expansion moves, notably into the UK, came at this time. The new cruiserweight ranges had appeared in 1970 and the launch of the 2800 series was then imminent. All these ventures cost money.

There was also another relevant factor. DAF had called in Knight-Wegenstein, the international Swiss firm of management consultants, in 1971 to advise the management on the best future structure of the company. They advised that the company should be split in two, with cars forming one company and trucks the other. This advice was followed and DAF Personenwagen BV (DAF Cars) and DAF Bedrÿfswagen BV (DAF Trucks) were the result. On the car side the company continued until its sale to Volvo at the beginning of 1976.

Then there were the company's engine developments and DAF's participation in the Club of Four light-truck design plan that had been embarked on just before this time. The European Truck Design programme, to give the Club of Four venture its proper name, was — as will be indicated in Chapter 5 — an agreement involving DAF, Magirus Deutz,

Saviem and Volvo for the joint development and testing of a light-truck range in the 6 to 12 tonnes gross weight bracket. A cab design common to all was envisaged, along with certain other shared features, but with the notable exceptions of the engine and power train. The individual manufacturers were left to come up with their own designs and the marketing of them.

Meanwhile, DAF's heavy expenditure and ambitious expansion programme in the early-1970s, even with IH's support, very nearly resulted in disaster, for 1974, and to some extent 1975, proved a period of recession for vehicle manufacture in Europe and DAF made a loss. Fortunately, the market then picked up and the next years were good ones.

DAF in the 1970s was becoming even more aware than ever of the need to keep close contact with the users of its vehicles. Aids to operators were increasingly introduced and included the DAF International Truck Service, a scheme offering instant assistance and credit facilities in the event of breakdown in all West European countries. A special ITS booklet was introduced giving the ITS telephone number in

Eindhoven and details of service centres throughout Europe and the Middle East.

DAF also developed maintenance systems for users to reduce the number of maintenance days, particularly in the case of vehicles with high annual mileages. A wealth of experience obtained by various operators was gathered together by DAF and then used to draw up the maintenance instructions, in close consultation with the vehicle designers. The systems were based on the concept that trucks operated in widely differing conditions and therefore needed a maintenance system adapted to the operating conditions. The conditions in which a vehicle operated on international haulage were, DAF pointed out, obviously different from and, from the point of view of maintenance, much more favourable than those encountered by a truck used on intensive in-town carrier service. Annual mileages also varied, and so four different maintenance systems were offered, based on the expected annual mileage.

The first system was intended for trucks covering less than 50,000 km a year, the second for the category covering 50,000-100,000 km a year, the third one for annual running from 100,000-150,000 km and the fourth one for those totalling more than 150,000 km a year.

It was left to the user to decide, in consultation with his dealer, which of the four systems he would adapt for a particular vehicle, and a separate maintenance booklet was made available for each system. The differences between the various systems were to be found in the intervals between such maintenance jobs as changing the oil in the engine, gearbox and axle or axles, renewing or cleaning the various filters and checking and adjusting the brakes and electrical components. Diagnostic equipment was also introduced throughout the DAF organization as an aid to this scheme, including a smoke meter diagnosis to enable the condition of the fuel-injection system to be determined, and equipment to check the electrical system.

A system of maintenance and repair contracts for the buyers of new vehicles was also evolved. This was part of a move to try to make transport operators more cost-conscious. DAF's stand at the 1976 Amsterdam Show had as its dominant theme cost control for hauliers. The company used

Mr Piet van Doorne, who is the present chairman of the Board of Management of DAF.

cost columns to depict the variable costs which have a major effect on the difference between purchase price and the selling price of transport per tonne/km and therefore on profit.

Subjects touched upon included increased efficiency by providing a good work environment for the driver and a high residual value, thus cutting interest charges and depreciation, a favourable vehicle weight/payload ratio and the lowest possible fuel consumption.

DAF also started to make a name for itself for its publicity activities, largely in connection with sporting occasions, first of all with football and then with sponsorships of other sports. These events ranged from sponsoring a cycling team in European championships, including the Tour de France, to boxing and motorcycling, sports in which DAF sponsored two world middleweight boxing championships and Britain's top motorcycle rider, Barry Sheene.

It was in September 1979 that the next major development

occurred in the company's history. A link between DAF Trucks and Dodge's European trucks operations (PSA Peugeot-Citroen Group) was mooted. The two companies announced that they were examining possibilities of technical and manufacturing co-operation in the truck sector. In a joint statement, they said that the main objective of the study was to consider various forms of co-operation ranging from an exchange of certain components to the future development of common components, using the existing resources of both parties to their mutual benefit.

Announcements of this kind invariably provide an opportunity to say something about the company, and this one was no exception. The statement made gave a useful picture of DAF as the 1970s drew to a close.

It was explained that DAF manufactured a range of diesel engines, front and rear axles and cabs for their commercial vehicles in their plants at Eindhoven, in the Netherlands, and Oevel, in Belgium. Dodge Trucks Europe, on the other hand, manufactured diesel engines, gearboxes, front and rear axles and cabs for their commercial vehicles at their plants at Dunstable and Luton, in England, and in Madrid, in Spain. DAF built vehicles in a range from 7 tonnes gross vehicle weight to 56 tonnes gross combination weight, Dodge from 3½ to 38 tonnes. A first evaluation of the existing facilities and products indicated component manufacturing as the main field of likely co-operation, it was stated.

As for the basic statistics, DAF employed approximately 9,100 people and produced 11,300 commercial vehicles in

DAF's cab-manufacturing plant is at Oeval, where this photograph of the assembly line was taken in 1973.

The DAF assembly line in Eindhoven in 1973, with a chassis and cab undergoing a final inspection before being driven away.

Oeval is the centre of DAF's axle production. This photograph taken in 1973 shows a rear axle and brake assembly nearing completion on the line.

1978, whilst the framework of ownership of the company was that van Doorne's Holding Company (Vado Beheer) held 42 per cent of the shares of DAF with International Harvester Company having a 33 per cent interest and the Dutch state-owned company DSM holding 25 per cent.

As part of the original DAF-IH agreement, however, IH in September 1980 exercised its option to take up a further 4½ per cent holding in DAF from the van Doorne holding company to give IH a 37½ per cent stake.

A landmark in the mid-1970s was, of course, the construction of the new headquarters office building and factory extension at Eindhoven, which gave a new look to the Eindhoven complex. Both the founders of the company, Hub and Wim, lived to see this, but not for long for Wim died at the age of 72 in 1978 and Hub a year later at 79, to end an exciting and eventful chapter in the company's history.

When the loss-making trailer plant was closed in 1979, the total plant complex was re-organized although some aspects remained untouched. The structure in 1980 was as follows:

The original 1930 plant, DAF 1, was occupied by the machine shop of the Special Products Division. DAF 2 remained as the main chassis plant with its own machine shop for components manufacture, the engine shop (with engine test facilities), the press shop handling all pressing, cutting and welding and the assembly line. Along the road at Geldrop (DAF 2) there was also the Special Vehicles Facility and the Military Product Group, and front and rear axles continued to be built at Oevel, in Belgium, where cabs were assembled and finished.

Mr Piet van Doorne commented on DAF's progress before the 1980 Amsterdam Show. He said that the company had started 1980 with a well-filled order book, extremely low levels of stocks and a good cash position. It had been decided to expand the company's technical production capacity —

DAF's cab and axle plant at Oeval seen from the air amidst characteristically flat countryside.

16,000 units annually — with only a marginal increase in personnel.

More than 15,000 vehicles were delivered to customers in 1979, a company record; actual production was 15,123 vehicles, including 1,000 buses.

Speaking about DAF's activities in the environmental sector, Mr van Doorne reported that in 1979 much attention was devoted to further improvement of working conditions, the emphasis being on combatting noise. A number of projects which would ultimately cost 1 million guilders were being implemented. For 1980, 2.3 million guilders had also been budgeted for activities in the field of safety, environmental protection and ergonomics, 900,000 guilders more than in 1979. The contingencies fund for this field, with equal representation of interested parties, amounted to 1 million guilders in 1980, compared with 500,000 guilders in the previous year.

Mr van Doorne revealed that the facilities at the company's proving ground at St Oedenrode were to be expanded, expenditure of 1.4 million guilders having been approved for the first phase, the construction of a driving circuit with a braking lane. In the subsequent four phases the proving ground would be developed into a modern complex, he promised.

Another major investment was in a new paint installation at the Eindhoven plant. This new installation, representing an investment of 8.5 million guilders, was designed to enable the company, by two-shifts working, to achieve a capacity sufficient to paint parts for 20,000 vehicles compared with the then-existing capacity of 14,000 units in three shifts.

Mr van Doorne had this to say about the prospects for 1980: 'The truck market was very buoyant last year. However, we must bear in mind that the increased demand was not so much a sign of a strong recovery from the weak economic situation that has existed for several years, but was rather the result of pent-up demand. This demand arose because our customers had had to observe a very cautious purchasing policy for a long time. The higher rates of inflation in Europe the last few months, the high interest rates and the continual increases in energy prices certainly do not promote further economic recovery.

'In view of the close link between truck sales and the state of the economy, we believe that we have several lean years ahead of us. Considering, furthermore, the surplus capacity of the European truck makers and the competition from the USA and Japan, it is quite clear that a hard battle will have to be fought.'

He mentioned, moreover, that he expected this Japanese and US competition to be encountered most severely in such places as northern Africa. In the short term, he did not fear Japanese competition in Europe, but after about 1985, the situation might be different, he added. He foresaw opportunities for growth in Spain, Italy and Greece, particularly when Spain and Greece entered the Common Market.

Mr van Doorne concluded his remarks with a forecast that

One of DAF's main pre-occupations in the 1970s was engine development. This is the engine-testing centre, with the offices of the test engineers in the foreground and the testing rooms with intake towers and separate exhaust systems behind.

Extensive testing of different makes and types of fuel pump is carried out as part of the engine-development programme.

Engines are tested thoroughly with the control room accurately monitoring engine behaviour with the aid of sophisticated checking and measuring equipment.

The performance of complete vehicles can be checked on chassis brake dynamometers.

DAF products, because of the company's improved sales and service organization, would do slightly better in 1980 than in 1979. When, later in the year, DAF's results were announced, it was revealed that the company had turned its 1978 loss to a 1979 profit through an increase of more than 30 per cent in sales. The company's 1979 turnover was 1,535,690,000 Dutch guilders. Net profit was 21,661,000 guilders in 1979 (against a net loss of 15,960,000 guilders in 1978).

DAF said that these favourable results were due to a much better performance in the commercial vehicle sector and were achieved in spite of a loss-making situation at DAF Special Products Division and the De Vleeschouwer foundry in Belgium. DAF Special Products was put on a sounder basis by the decision in mid-1979 to wind-up the trailer and semi-trailer operations at Eindhoven and in Spain. It had also been decided to close the loss-making foundry by mid-1980 at the latest.

The company produced 15,123 vehicles in 1979 (against 11,371 units in 1978) but even this all-time record output fell

An engine being prepared for a series of performance tests in the engine-dynamometer cell.

Another example of the DAF — International Harvester association was this 1972 picture of the International Paystar 5000 6 × 4 tipper which was fitted with the DAF DKA 1160 engine rated at 230 bhp (DIN).

short of the market requirements, commented the company. With record deliveries to customers of 15,547 vehicles (against 11,629 units in 1978), the sales organization had a well-filled order book and a low stock of vehicles at the end of 1979. DAF gave its views about this: 'The Board of Management believes that the buoyancy of total commercial vehicle sales in most countries of Western Europe in 1979 was due virtually solely to the release of pent-up demand. It could hardly have been caused by the level of economic activities, which showed only a modest increase.'

To increase the sales potential outside existing markets and reduce the dependence on European markets, the company has opened area offices in the Middle East (Dubai), Africa (Abidjan) and Scandinavia (Gothenburg). These offices, says DAF, will enable the markets to be served better, and the initial results are satisfactory. In Sweden, DAF Trucks has started building up a sales and service organization of its own.

In 1979, DAF Trucks spent 45,516,000 guilders on investment for product improvement, product development in the longer term and strengthening of the international sales organization. Investment in 1978 totalled 41,896,000 guilders.

The number of employees of the total DAF Trucks organization increased by more than 200 to almost 9,400 in 1979. There were increases at the Eindhoven and Oevel plants on account of the higher production levels.

Speaking about prospects for 1980, DAF said that since

Testing a bonneted N 2800 series on the torsion track at St Oedenrode.

uncertain economic factors continued to prevail and developments in Western European markets were expected to vary quite considerably, 'the Board of Management finds it difficult to make a reliable forecast. If the economy does not show a clear improvement in 1980 and the pent-up demand is fully met, there would seem to be some lean years ahead in view of the existing over-capacity in the commercial vehicle industry. DAF Trucks, however, started 1980 with a number of advantages, such as a well-filled order book and a low stock of vehicles.'

Test facilities at DAF's test track at St Oedenrode, near Eindhoven, received a boost in December 1980 when a completely soundproofed hall went into use to study and analyze noise sources in vehicles, and to determine the effect

Chassis frame torsion-testing on the N 2800 series at Eindhoven.

of any constructional changes on the noise level.

The test complex was due for completion early in 1981, with sections for functional tests, hill sections, skid pads, a water trough for wading tests, high-pressure douches to test dust and water-tightness, and a circuit where the off-road qualities of vehicles can be tested.

Work on the St Oedenrode test facilities has progressed steadily since 1971, when the site was first purchased. A copy of a Belgian pavé road, 3 km long, was built first in 1971, and to prevent distortion of the surface the cobbles were set in concrete. A steering pad was built in 1973, with a range of surfaces and equipment to simulate rain. This is used for steering effort measurement, 'emergency steering' characteristics, lateral-stability measurement and for testing handling.

A crash track came into use in 1975, suitable for speeds up to 50 km/h, and there is a section for measuring noise. A torsion track of steel angle went into service in 1978 for testing the torsional stiffness of chassis frames, vehicle suspensions, shock absorber adjustment and the torsional loading of chassis frames with auxiliary frame and bodywork.

Then, in 1979, a section was built for high-speed testing

(90-120 km/h). This section facilitates a great number of tests, such as roadholding and steering characteristics, emergency braking characteristics, deceleration measurement, brake-fade testing, jack-knifing of vehicle combinations, and fuel consumption, towing, tyre and acceleration tests.

Chapter 3

The military vehicle rôle

When DAF produced the Trado in the 1930s the seal was set on the company as a manufacturer of military vehicles, production of which was to be of particular importance in the formative years of the early-1950s. In fact, the number of military vehicles exceeded those built for civilian use every year until the end of 1958.

Today, of course, the position is totally different, for DAF is concentrating almost completely on commercial vehicle manufacture, with its military vehicle production never exceeding 10 per cent of total build. Nevertheless, the company has a name in military vehicle construction so it is appropriate to devote a chapter to this sector of its activities.

The basis of DAF as a military vehicle builder was a very big order, worth 175 million guilders, funded under the Marshall Aid programme and placed shortly after the postwar factory opening.

The first powered military vehicle in this programme was the YA 318, a 3 tonnes payload, 6 tonnes gross, 6 × 6. This, however, was soon replaced by the YA 328, an improved version of the YA 318, which was produced as a general-purpose truck and as an artillery tractor. There was little difference between the two versions, the main one being that the general-purpose vehicle had a body 20 in (500 mm) longer than that on the gun tractor.

The six-wheel-driven YA 328 was a forward-control vehicle fitted with the Hercules six-cylinder petrol engine, which had a maximum torque of 270 lb ft at 1,400 rpm. This power unit was matched with a five-speed constant-mesh gearbox used in combination with a two-speed transfer box for negotiating particularly difficult terrain.

Although fitted with a standard canvas tilt-covered, all-steel body, the driving cab was open to the skies, but with a divided windscreen. The driver and co-driver were protected from the elements by a canvas hood, which buttoned down on to the top of the windscreen. A feature of the body design was that the wheelarches were extended so that, when fitted with removable wooden slats, they could be used for seats by personnel. When not in use as seats, these slats could be placed across the wheelarches to form a flat loading platform.

A special feature of this vehicle when used as a gun tractor was that a winch of DAF's own design was mounted under the body between the main chassis members. Controlled from the driver's seat, this winch was fitted with a 165 ft (50 m) long cable and equipped with a torque-limiting device. An automatic pintle hook at the rear of the vehicle was attached to this winch cable.

This was the biggest military vehicle produced by DAF in this period and it had several features which the designers also incorporated in two other models which were built at the same time — the ¼-tonne payload 4 × 4 model YA 054, a general-purpose truck, and the 1-tonne payload 4 × 4 YA 126, which was supplied in several forms as a weapon carrier, staff car or ambulance. The characteristics of all these vehicles were good ground clearance, independent suspension

The extent of DAF's involvement in military vehicle production is revealed in this 1958 photograph of a military transport exhibition. The majority of the vehicles seen here were built by DAF. Throughout the 1950s until this time, military vehicle production had exceeded that of construction for civilian use.

on all wheels and a transmission layout common to all designs, including one central differential.

The YA 054 ¼-tonne 4 × 4 was fitted with the Hercules four-cylinder petrol engine producing 60 bhp at 3,200 rpm and a maximum torque of 138 lb ft at 1,400 rpm. A three-speed synchromesh gearbox provided the main transmission in this instance, supplemented by a two-speed transfer box in which, since the vehicle was basically front-wheel driven, the rear-wheel drive could be disengaged. The all-steel body was open and had a fold-down windscreen and it was, in effect, DAF's answer to the Jeep, many of which were still to be found all over Europe as part of the huge legacy of war surplus equipment left by the Allied forces.

The YA 126 1-tonner had the Hercules six-cylinder petrol engine, in this case rated at 103 bhp at 3,200 rpm and delivering a maximum torque of 207 lb ft at 1,400 rpm. As with the ¼-tonne vehicle, the gearbox was a synchromesh unit, although in this instance it had four forward speeds, and

the transfer box, again a two-speed unit, permitted disengagement of the front-wheel drive as the vehicle was rear-axle-driven. A canvas tilt covered the all-steel body, an extension flap buttoning down on the top of the vehicle's windscreen to provide weather protection for the driver.

All these original DAF military vehicle designs had a similar transmission layout. The gearbox (synchromesh or constant-mesh) was mounted directly to the engine with the power going through a short transmission shaft to a transfer box (always with the two ratios) mounted centrally in the chassis frame. The transfer case housing also contained the central differential from which short axles drove bevel boxes to transmit power to the extremely short stub-axles driving the front and rear axles.

DAF's military vehicle role at this time was not confined to powered vehicles and its trailer-making traditions found expression in the construction of an aircraft refuelling semi-trailer, the YF 101. This had a box-shaped chassis with

The component parts of DAF's pre-World War 2 Trado system for converting a conventional 4 × 2 truck into a 6 × 4. It featured longitudinal swinging rockers with stub-axles geared to the normal differential.

commercial vehicle production levels started to exceed those of military vehicles there was a total shift of emphasis at DAF from the purpose-built military vehicle to those adapted from its basic commercial vehicle designs.

DAF's Trado design showing its fitment on a pre-World War 2 Ford chassis in which use was made of the existing drive-line to effect the conversion to drive all four rear wheels.

welded cross-members shaped to take the special tank which was a one-compartment, all-welded, 2,240 gallon (Imperial) capacity design with a separate compartment at the rear to house filters, meter and valves.

All the equipment on the trailer was made by DAF; it had a DAF tandem axle as its running gear with special laminated springs of DAF's own design, there was a DAF fifth wheel, and even the brakes were DAF's own powerful vacuum units. Swinging booms, also mounted at the rear, permitted easy loading of the fuel; it took just three minutes to load a jet fighter with 2,300 litres of kerosene.

In this period of the 1950s, DAF also supplied large numbers of small trailers for NATO. The aircraft refuellers were built not only for the Dutch forces, but also for those of a number of other countries, including Norway and Denmark. It was a time of steady development, with the company moving up the weight scale in 1956 with the introduction of the YA 616, a 6 × 6 6-tonner, which was built in a variety of forms, including general-purpose units, tippers, command offices, tractor units and wreckers. As

A Ford V8-engined military scout car fitted with the Trado system. Note the tiny wheels fitted both to the front and to the rear of the front axle to help the vehicle over hillocks.

A 1938/39 Ford light truck, fitted with the Trado rear axle, showing its articulating qualities over rough country when hauling a drawbar trailer.

There were exceptions, however, a notable one being the twin-steering 8 × 8 YP 408 developed in the 1960s for the Dutch forces. This made its greatest impact as an armoured car, although it also went into service as a general-purpose troop-carrying gun tractor, command post and ambulance. DAF experimented with an amphibious vehicle at this time, but in fact it was not the first amphibian to be built by DAF. A remarkable little vehicle called the MC 139 amphibian was built before World War 2, which had a driving seat at both front and rear so that it could be driven easily in either direction — not at the same time, of course!

It was in the 1960s, too, that a prototype of a small purpose-built military vehicle, called the DAF Pony, was built. This was the YP 500, which was built as a flat-platform load-carrier — with balloon tyres and just a seat, steering column and foot controls — which could be parachuted from an aircraft. It was a design which employed the flat-twin-cylinder DAF engine and the Variomatic transmission used in DAF cars. Apart from these somewhat unusual vehicles, any glance at the military vehicles built from the 1960s onwards

DAF's military vehicle interests in the 1950s were not without previous involvement in this type of vehicle. This photograph shows the factory in the 1930s with Ford light truck chassis awaiting fitment with the Trado.

A prototype amphibious vehicle built by DAF for the Dutch Army just before World War 2. It had a driver's seat at both the front and rear of the vehicle so that it could be driven (or steered) in either direction without having to be turned round.

DAF's Trado design on a Ford chassis in use in boggy country as a light personnel carrier and gun tractor.

Developed in the 1960s, the YA 314 four-wheeled truck was the main workhorse for the Dutch Army until it was replaced by the YA 4440.

increasingly reflected their commercial vehicle origins.

DAF by this time had got itself some admirers in military vehicle terms outside the Netherlands and it was in 1966 that DAF granted a licence to ENASA (Pegaso) in Spain to build a more powerful version of its YA 314, 3-tonne truck. The Pegaso-built design was the YA 414 3045, which it started to build in 1970 using DAF components at first, including the DAF 135 bhp six-cylinder petrol engine, but later using an increasing number of Pegaso components, including its own 125 bhp diesel engine, which itself was derived from a Leyland unit. A derivative of this vehicle is still being built — as a Pegaso, the DAF licence agreement having run out in 1976.

Another overseas admirer is the Brazilian Engesa concern, which has successfully fitted the DAF military rear

The air-portable Pony was developed by the company in the 1960s for the NATO forces. It featured the Variomatic belt-drive transmission of the type used in the DAF car.

DAF's YP 408 armoured car, developed in the 1960s, was an 8 × 8 design with all axles steering. The company no longer produces vehicles of this kind.

One of DAF's most popular models of the 1950s was the YA 328 6 × 6 3-tonner, which was offered as a gun tractor or, with slightly longer body, as a personnel carrier. It had a Hercules six-cylinder petrol engine and a five-speed gearbox.

suspension design (Trado System) which Engesa call Boomerang. It is fitted on Engesa's EE.25 military truck, which it has been selling not only to the Brazilian armed forces but also overseas; more than 1,000 have been exported by the Brazilian company.

The general-purpose military vehicles built by DAF in the 1950s lasted through the 1960s, supplemented by the additions mentioned, and it was not until the 1970s that totally new models replaced some of the ageing designs. However, not all of these new designs turned out to be what was required — not through the fault of DAF, but from changing military requirements. Thus, for example, the YA 2442 4 × 4, developed as a 2-tonner for the Dutch Army in the early-1970s and subjected to extensive trials and tests, did not turn out to be the vehicle that was really wanted, although another similar vehicle was right. This was the YA 4440 which was to be the main vehicle for the 1980s. It is both more versatile than the YA 2442 and offers greater load capacity.

The YA 4440 is replacing the YA 314 and YA 328 trucks supplied by DAF Trucks to the Dutch Army in the 1950s. Unlike its predecessors, the YA 4440 is fitted with a diesel engine, so that in due course most of the Army's fleet of vehicles will be running on diesel fuel. It was put on display at the RAI Show in Amsterdam in 1978, but not exactly as a new model, for the Dutch Ministry of Defence had ordered 4,000 trucks of this type at the end of 1976, after putting several prototypes through exhaustive tests. A repeat order for a further 2,500 trucks was placed at the end of 1977.

A drawing of the YA 328 6 × 6 military chassis which went into service in the 1950s with the Dutch Army.

Although the YA 4440 is a 4-tonne truck designed for military operation and thus complies with military requirements, it reflects current DAF policy in that it incorporates a large number of components from DAF's normal commercial vehicles. Fitted with the DAF DT615 turbocharged six-cylinder diesel engine, this vehicle is certainly not short of power. It has an output of 113 kW (153 bhp) on the DIN-EEC scale which, with a kerb-weight of 6,650 kg, gives it a power-to-weight ratio of close to 14.2 bhp per tonne. Maximum torque is a useful 372 lb ft at 1,400 rpm. The rest of the power train consists of the German ZF S5 35/2 five-speed synchromesh gearbox and ZF VG 250/2 transfer case, which permits front-wheel drive to be engaged or disengaged as required. Both the axles are of DAF's own

design, the front being the 2235V 6-tonnes design and the rear the 6.5-tonnes DAF 1635, a fully floating single-speed unit. Front and rear axle ratios are the same at 5.72:1.

The performance which results from this is impressive. Top-speed capability is 87 km/h as a solo vehicle and it can cope with a gradient of 50 per cent or, when pulling a 4-tonnes payload trailer, 20 per cent. Like the gearboxes, the steering gear is also of ZF design, in this case the ZF 8042, a power-assisted unit, of course. With a vehicle length of 7.05 m, width of 2.44 m, wheelbase of 4.05 m and track of 1.91 m, it offers a turning circle of 18 m.

Although the ground clearance is 0.3 m, the equipment attached to the chassis itself is well off the ground to afford a clearance of 0.55 m around the vehicle's centre-line. The

DAF's YA 4440 model, which is derived from its commercial vehicle designs and thus uses a high proportion of common components, has excellent mobility characteristics in all types of terrain, as shown here.

Full two-line dual-circuit air brakes with load-sensing device are fitted and the parking brake is a lever-actuated unit operating on the front axle. An exhaust brake is also standard, as is a trailer brake connection. The two-seat tilt cab fitted has a reinforced roof to permit the installation of a ring mounting for a light machine gun, the frame supporting the ring being bolted directly to the cab roof over the manhole cover.

DAF offers a wide range of variations in both right and left-hand-drive form to the basic design of the YA 4440 so, for example, an automatic transmission can be fitted if desired; also available are a third seat in the cab, and variations in lighting, instruments, tyres and items to meet specific safety regulations. It is also possible to have special equipment fitted like an hydraulic 1-tonne loading and unloading crane, in which case the loading deck can be pierced with the holes necessary for the crane's installation.

The second main military vehicle in this phase of development is the YA 5441. Like the 4-tonner, this is a standard general-purpose 5-tonne design with an identical power train to the YA 4440. Axles and suspension are also identical, but 7.0—20 wheels (twins on the rear axle) with 10.00—20 XL, 16-ply radial cross-country tyres are fitted on the 5-tonner against the 8.0—20 wheels (singles on the rear axle) with 12.00—20 non-directional tyres forming the footwear of the 4-tonners.

The main variations otherwise lie in the dimensions. The 5-tonner is longer at 7.5 m, but at 2.32 m it is narrower. Yet the wheelbase is shorter at 3.85 m and the track at the front is 1.94 m and at the rear 1.73 m. Turning circle is a tighter 16.5 m. As a result of the dimensional differences there is a big variation in axle weights, 4.9 tonnes on the front axle of the 5-tonner (1.1 tonnes less than the 4-tonne version) and 8.1 tonnes on the rear axle (6.5 tonnes). Ground clearance under axles becomes 0.27 m and under chassis 0.45 m. Kerb weight is 7.29 tonnes. All these changes generate a different performance for the 5-tonner. Maximum speed drops to 80 km/h and gradient capability without trailer is rather better than 59 per cent; with laden trailer it becomes 38 per cent. The angle of approach is shallower at 32 degrees, as is the angle of departure at 23 degrees; wading depth is

angle of approach is 41 degrees and angle of departure 30 degrees, maximum tilt angle is 30 degrees and the wading depth is 0.9 m. DAF stresses that special attention has been paid to the construction of the vehicle's suspension and of its bodywork. The suspension is of conventional design with semi-elliptic springs supplemented by double-acting, telescopic hydraulic shock absorbers front and rear. The body,. especially the load platform, has great torsional stiffness, with four-point mounting protecting the body against undue racking of the chassis during off-road operations.

DAF's military YA 4440, introduced in 1977, was shown to the public for the first time at the Amsterdam Show of 1978. It is a 4-tonne design which incorporates a large number of components from DAF's normal commercial vehicle models.

Although DAF closed down its trailer-making activities in 1979, it can still produce specials, like this YTS 10050 tank transporter, through its special-vehicle production unit.

A low deck height is a feature of this particular vehicle in the military series for the 1980s. The cab is very noticeably derived from DAF's current commercial vehicle design.

substantially less at 0.6 m.

Throughout the 1960s and 1970s DAF continued its trailer-making and bodybuilding activities, with aircraft refuellers on both rigid and articulated outfits being a main speciality. The designs had a capability to draw off fuel from aircraft as well as pump it into the tanks. They also incorporated automatic fire-fighting systems. Purpose-designed tank-transporting semi-trailers were another speciality, and their production has not been entirely abandoned.

In 1979, when DAF finally closed down its trailer-making operation, some of its activities were continued through a Special Vehicle Production Unit at Eindhoven. This, for example, can turn out the popular DAF YTS 10050 tank-transporter trailer. Built for transporting virtually any type of tracked vehicle of up to 55 tonnes in weight, this design is in use in the Belgian, Danish, Swedish and Dutch armed forces. Its extensive specification includes removable chocks, mooring eyes and lashing rings to hold the equipment being carried on the trailer. It has twin-winch cable pulleys mounted on the swan neck of the trailer to facilitate the loading or unloading of broken-down vehicles, the winches themselves being mounted on the hauling vehicle.

The running gear of the trailer consists of two sets of oscillating tandem-axle units, positioned side-by-side. Each of these units comprises a rocker beam, centrally suspended without springs from the chassis frame. The rocker beam has two longitudinal axle-shafts supported on self-adjusting ball-bushings. A stub-axle, with wheels, hubs and brake drums, is attached to the outer end of each longitudinal axle-shaft. Each wheel brake is applied separately by an air-brake chamber located between the wheels to reduce the risk of damage. Two wide ramps are fitted at the rear, each one being pivot-mounted and incorporating adjustable supports. When not in use the ramps and supports are raised and locked to the chassis frame.

Through its Special Vehicle Production Unit, DAF can, of

A variety of bodywork is feasible in the DAF military vehicle series. This tilt-bodied YA 4440 model is also equipped with high flotation cross-country tyres.

course, build other special types of trailer — and powered vehicles — if required. Any such inquiry is treated on its merits and of course has to be commercially worthwhile. Moreover, it should not be overlooked that many DAF commercial vehicles, such as its tractor units, can readily be used for military purposes with basically little modification to the specification. Obviously, such things as tyre equipment and the fitment of accessories and options requires little deviation from normal production practice. The disappearance of the trailer-manufacturing function does, however, mean that DAF will no longer have the same involvement as hitherto in the supply of such vehicles as

aircraft refuelling tankers, which were one of the specialities of this division.

Currently, DAF endeavours to keep military production to a maximum of 10 per cent of the total build. It is in the process of developing a general-purpose 6 × 6 10-tonner for the Dutch forces, which could form part of the next Dutch vehicle replacement programme. In the meantime, the company is working on a production programme which is due for completion in 1982, by which date, DAF will have supplied 6,500 of the YA 4440. The 6 × 6 will supplement rather than replace them.

The best sellers — Military Vehicles — the YA 4440

Type:	YA 4440, 4 × 4, payload 4 tonnes, kerb-weight 6.65 tonnes.	Steering gear:	ZF 8042, hydraulically-assisted.
Engine:	DAF DT 615, turbocharged direct-injection six-cylinder diesel, output 153 bhp on DIN-EEC scale.	Brakes:	Dual-circuit air, plus exhaust brake.
		Suspension:	Semi-elliptic springs and shock absorbers.
Gearbox:	ZF S 5-35/2, five-speed synchromesh gearbox.	Electrical system:	24V.
Transfer case:	ZF VG 250/2.	Cab:	Two-seater tilt cab.
Overall length:	7.05 m.	Performance:	Maximum speed — approx. 87 km/h;
Wheelbase:	4.05 m.		minimum speed — approx. 3.5 km/h;
Front axle:	DAF 2235 V, capacity 6 tonnes.		gradeability — approx. 50 per cent;
Rear axle:	DAF 1635, capacity 6.5 tonnes.		fordability — approx. 0.90 m;
			operating range — approx. 600 km.

Chapter 4

Vehicles of the 1960s

The early-1960s proved a key period for DAF. Until then the company could not be termed a manufacturer of ultra-heavies, but Dutch legislation changes were to alter this completely, for this was the time when weight limits were raised in the Netherlands to permit articulated vehicles to run at weights of up to 34 tonnes, and it was not to be long before higher weights than these would be permitted, subject to semi-trailer axle-spread and bogie-weight requirements.

It was obvious to everyone in the Netherlands, not least the Government, that there was a rosy future for international haulage and that Dutch hauliers, with Rotterdam — Europe's leading seaport — and Amsterdam within its frontiers and Antwerp — Europe's second biggest port — just outside them, were in a strong position to gain substantially from international long-distance haulage movements.

In 1957 the all-important Transport International Routiers (TIR) Customs Convention had been signed whereby vehicles of an approved design could pass freely under TIR customs seal across frontiers without being opened-up for inspection. Roll-on, roll-off ferry services, initially between Britain and Continental Europe, were starting to appear, although they were not as yet widely used.

There was, however, a traffic explosion to come with a second, even more important development for the Netherlands to follow in the mid-1960s — the freight container revolution. This was, perhaps, of greater significance to the Netherlands than any other country for Rotterdam was to become the focal point in Europe, first for the deep-sea container traffic on the North American routes, and then for short-sea movements between Great Britain and Ireland and Continental Europe. With Antwerp and Amsterdam also proving popular as European terminals for these classes of shipment, everything was set fair for Dutch hauliers for a massive road-transport boom. It was logical for the home vehicle manufacturer — DAF — to take advantage of this, and the Dutch Government had the foresight to push through the legislation which gave them the right tools to do so.

In terms of hardware, the 1960s for DAF can be seen as a time of steady progression up the weight scale with ever-improving designs, but ones influenced heavily on the one hand by the need for vehicles to run internationally rather than domestically and, in domestic terms, to handle the movement of freight containers of 20ft to 30ft or 40ft long and weighing up to 30 imperial tons.

As indicated at the end of the opening chapter, DAF moved into the 1960s with what were then three new models — the 1500, 1600 and 1800 series. The growing significance of international haulage, however, was reflected by the introduction in the 1960/61 model programme of a 2000 series vehicle fitted with a sleeper cab — DAF's first.

These were not to be the models that carved for DAF a permanent place in the history of international haulage. This was to come in 1962, when the company unveiled the models

Three examples of the 2000-series range, which was introduced in 1960. The 2200 series, which was an extension of it, was announced at the same time.

One of the first 2600-series models, which entered service in 1962. Introduced primarily for international haulage, it was equipped with the advanced new fixed cab and was powered by the Leyland 0.680 diesel engine.

built to meet the then new Dutch higher weight limits, the flagship of the range being the 2600 model fitted with the Leyland 0.680 engine producing 220 bhp on the SAE scale. The vehicle had a new cab design, a fixed as opposed to tilt unit, which already showed some of the characteristics that were to give DAF a sound name in cab design in the years to come. It had other advanced concepts for those days, notably power-assisted steering, which was installed as a standard fitment, as were air brakes.

Fitment of either a 10-tonne or a 13-tonne axle was possible on the new 1800 and 1900 series introduced at this time. The 10-tonne axle gave a Dutch vehicle a maximum gross weight of 16 tonnes, but the 13-tonne axle could be fitted on vehicles intended for Belgium and France where, respectively, 17-tonne and 19-tonne gross four-wheelers were legally permitted. A specially-strengthened 4 × 2 tipper chassis was introduced, as was a 6 × 2 chassis for general haulage and a 4 × 2 purpose-built to take a concrete-mixing body.

The Dutch legal changes did not end with the introduction of higher gross weight limits, and 1963 saw the 2300 series sandwiched in between the 2000 and 2600 models with axles rated at 11 tonnes (the new legal limit) replacing the 10-tonne units hitherto featured. At this time, too, DAF introduced its first ever 6 × 4 designs for tipper and concrete-mixer duties, the AT 1900/1902 models, which fitted the DAF turbocharged 575 S engine.

The ranges offered by DAF in the early-1960s reflected a marked step forward in the deliberate policy of DAF aimed at its target of making all its major components. DAF had, of course, started building its own cabs in 1953, but it was not until 1957 that its engine factory was opened, and 1958 that the company began building its own axles.

These developments bore fruit in the ranges introduced from 1959 onwards with DAF in a position to move up the weight scale in power terms with the availability of its DD 575 engine, producing 120 bhp, and its turbocharged DS 575, rated at 165 bhp at 2,400 rpm. Both of these power units turned out to be very reliable, the turbocharged unit doing extremely well in the T 1800 tractor unit models rated for gross combination weight operation at up to 28 tonnes, where it was matched with a six-speed constant-mesh gearbox or, as

an option, a synchromesh unit.

The same engine and power train combination was offered in the 1900 series, although here a rear axle rated at 10.6 tonnes with a ratio of 5.72 or 6.33:1 (according to model) was used instead of the 5.17:1 ratio of the 1800. A beefier front axle of 5.4 tonnes capacity in the 1900 series contrasted with the 4-tonne unit of the 1800 models.

The original 2000 DO series fitted the Leyland 0.680 engine, also rated at 165 bhp, but at 2,000 rpm, a range which had a load capacity of 14.8 tonnes gross vehicle weight in solo 4 × 2 form with a payload of 8 to 9 tonnes, although as an

When the 2600's cab received its first facelift in 1964, the result was this roomy, well-appointed and insulated work place for the driver, making it one of the most advanced cabs of its time.

Two versions of the extensively improved 1969 cab on the 2600 series showing, on the opposite page, the De Luxe version and, left, the Super Comfort model, the latter being distinguished by different trim, greater use of sound-deadening materials and a more comfortable passenger's seat.

articulated vehicle tractor unit it was rated at 35 tonnes gcw. A six-speed constant-mesh box was standard, with a synchromesh unit as an option, connected to a 10-tonne back axle. The 2000 DO series — with facelifted cab — was later uprated to a 16-tonne gross 4 × 2 solo load carrier and 28-32 tonnes gcw operation as an artic tractor unit. This coincided with the fitment of a more powerful version of the Leyland 0.680, rated at 180 bhp at 2,000 rpm. It had the same gearbox options as the 2000 DO series, but the standard back axle ratio was 5.14:1, a ratio which had been offered as an option on the earlier design where the standard was 4.62:1.

In effect, this revised 2000 DO model replaced only one

sector of the market held by the first 2000 DO series. This can be seen from its artic rating at 28-32 tonnes instead of the 35 tonnes of the earlier model. Later (in 1963), at the top end of the weight scale, the 2300 DO series took over, also fitting the facelifted cab of the 2000 series. In solo form the Leyland 0.680-powered 2300 4 × 2 was rated at 18.4 tonnes gross, a weight based on the use of a 5.4-tonne front axle and a 13-tonne rear unit. As an artic it had a gcw rating of 32-36 tonnes.

The fitment of the 13-tonne axles reflected that this was the vehicle built with the Belgian and French markets in mind and so constituting a landmark for DAF, hinting at the strong

of construction was employed for the main frame, with conventional semi-elliptic steel springs providing the basic suspension, supplemented on the front axle by double-acting telescopic shock absorbers. Dual-circuit air brakes and hydraulic power steering formed part of the specification, as it now did on all DAF designs.

Extra models were added to the 2600 series throughout the 1960s. The ability to fit 13-tonne capacity rear axles generated the models suitable for the Belgian and French markets to lift gvw rating on solo vehicles to 19 tonnes and the gcw rating on artic tractor units first to 36-40 tonnes and in 1968, when DAF produced its 250 bhp DKA 1160 six-cylinder diesel engine, the rating rose to 38-42 tonnes. The 1960s were thus a period of constant progress with all DAF ranges. From a mere handful of models, the ranges available increased steadily so that by 1970 the versions offered totalled 69.

There was quite an emphasis in the company's rigid models on vehicles for the construction industry. Accordingly, in 1965, the first 6 × 6 tipper chassis, the AZ 1900 DS, made its appearance, to be followed a year later by an extra-heavy-duty 6 × 4 for tipper duties in the French market. Other three-axled machines, a 6 × 2 and a 6 × 4, followed in the next year. As always, the Amsterdam Show, in this case in 1966, provided the showcase for these DAF developments. One of the most startling was a highly original air-and-leaf-spring suspension system on a bus chassis, a design concept which was later to be adopted in modified form on goods vehicles.

However, on the goods vehicle front proper, the show saw the 6 × 2 design mentioned earlier. Designed for haulage work at the maximum gross weight of 26 tonnes, the AS 2400, as it was termed, was based on the 2400 series of forward-control, four-wheel chassis and was equipped with a completely new trailing-axle assembly. In this, each of the trailing axle wheels was independently suspended on the rear end of a rocking beam, which itself pivotted on a special chassis cross-member. To ensure correct load distribution between the two bogie axles under all conditions, the forward end of each rocking beam was connected by a nearly vertical link to the rear end of a conventional semi-elliptic leaf spring bolted in the normal way to the driven axle. When fully laden,

move, from this time on, into the territories of neighbouring countries. This promise of expansion could also be seen especially in the 2600 series. In its early form this also had a Leyland engine, the uprated 0.680, now producing 220 bhp at 2,200 rpm, up 22 per cent on the 180 bhp version. A six-speed constant-mesh gearbox and double-reduction rear axle completed the power train. As a solo load carrier the 6-tonne front axle and 10-tonne rear gave the vehicle a gross weight of 16 tonnes whilst, as an artic tractor unit, a maximum gross combination weight of 32-36 tonnes was the designed weight, the same as the models fitting 13-tonne axles.

As with all DAF vehicles of the period, an all-welded form

the driving and trailing axles shared the bogie load in the proportion of ten to six. As optional equipment, a load-transfer device was offered to improve traction for the driving wheels on slippery surfaces and to allow the rearmost wheels to be raised clear of the road when running empty. During development work, single tyres were tried on the less heavily laden trailing wheels, but tread wear was found to be disproportionately high so, although singles were still offered, twin tyres were selected as standard equipment.

Amsterdam 1966 was a show of widely spread trailer bogies, the Dutch having introduced a law permitting 20 tonnes to be transmitted to the road surface if axles on a tandem bogie were 2.05 metres (6 ft 9 in) apart. DAF had a number of its trailer designs on view and used the exhibition to announce that in semi-trailer production it was moving over to semi-automatic production to speed-up deliveries. This involved the adoption of a standard method of construction using pierced main frames and full-width cross-members. DAF also brought out a two-axled version of the DAF 2400 at this time, which was available as a 4 × 4 for tipping work at 19 tonnes gvw. It employed the same mechanical components as the 2600 series.

1968 was to prove perhaps the most important year of the 1960s for DAF, because it was at the Amsterdam Show of that year that the 11.6-litre DAF engine was unveiled. It was to be the bedrock of DAF's expansion in the next decade. It is appropriate to pause and take a look at DAF engine development at this point, for 1968 marked DAF's complete switch to engines of its own manufacture.

Back in the early-1950s, DAF had been totally dependent

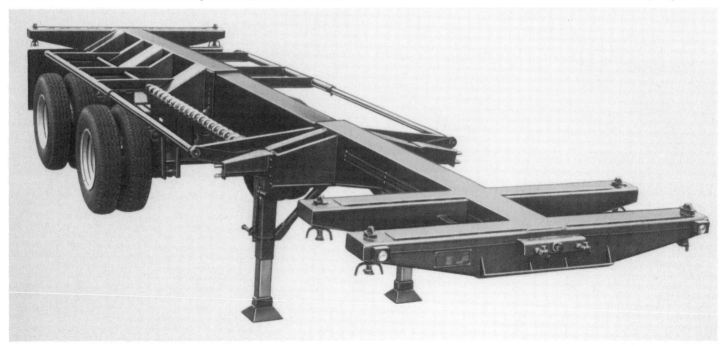

Trailer making was still big business for DAF in the 1960s. This shows an extendible semi-trailer built in 1969.

This was one of the first 2600-series vehicles with the much improved cab introduced in 1969.

on bought-in power units, initially Hercules petrol engines and Perkins diesels and later the Leyland 0.350, which DAF made under licence, and which was to form the basis of the DD 575 DAF engines. DAF made quite a few design modifications in making it into a DAF engine in its own right.

The first model had a maximum power output of 120 bhp at 2,400 rpm, compared with 105 bhp at the same rpm of the Leyland 0.350 that it replaced. Maximum torque was 38 mkg (275 lb ft) at 1,400 rpm compared with the Leyland's 253 lb ft at 1,400 rpm. The engine's capacity at 5.75 litres was the same as that of the 0.350 Leyland, as were the bore and stroke at 100.6 × 120.7mm and other salient features. Where the big difference came was in the development by DAF of its highly successful turbocharged version, the DS 575, which lifted the maximum output to 165 bhp at 2,400 rpm.

The next stage in this engine's development came with the announcement at the 1966 Amsterdam Show of the DF 615, a bored-out version of the DD 575, having a maximum power output of 126 bhp at 2,600 rpm and a maximum torque of 282 lb ft at 1,400 rpm. A Bosch fuel-injection pump with

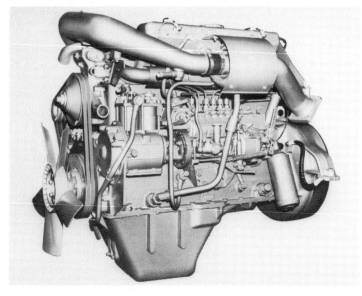

The DT 615 six-cylinder diesel engine was first produced in the 1960s. It is seen here in the form it took in the late-1970s, when, in turbocharged form, it produced 153 bhp at 2,400 rpm.

The DAF 11.6-litre diesel engine, developed in the 1960s, powered this 2000-series tractor unit seen here hauling one of DAF's aluminium alloy chassisless Eurotrailer semi-trailers.

Equipped with on-and-off-highway tyres, this short-wheelbase chassis was a popular choice for Dutch tipper operators in the 1960s.

A 1-tonne payload was feasible on the lightweight Pony chassis equipped with the DAF car engine and Variomatic transmission.

mechanical governor replaced the CAV unit on the DD 575 and a 14-inch clutch was required, as with the DS 575.

With heavier trucks in mind, DAF signed a second licence agreement with Leyland for the production of the Leyland O.680, 11.1-litre engine. It was this engine which formed the basis in 1968 of the range of DAF 11.6-litre engines used in its then heaviest-yet range of models. Three versions were unveiled, the DKD 1160 developing 165 bhp (DIN) at 2,000 rpm, the DK 1160 of 212 bhp at 2,200 rpm, and the DKA 1160, for use in 38-tonne gross outfits, producing 230 bhp at the same engine speed.

The DKA 1160 engine incorporated a special induction system, which used a number of stainless steel tubes of carefully calculated length and shape leading from a pressure equalizing box on the opposite side of the engine from the inlet ports. These had the function of taking the place of a conventional manifold and utilized the pressure fluctuations caused by the opening and closing of the inlet valves to give a pressure pulse at the moment before each valve closed. Volumetric efficiency was, therefore, increased from around 85 to 91 per cent.

In other respects these in-line six-cylinder engines were fairly orthodox and followed on from the Leylands save that a cross-flow cooling system was adopted to give constant

The DAF Pony is shown here as a tractor unit coupled to a semi-trailer for articulated-vehicle duties. It had a payload of 1½ tonnes.

operating temperature between cylinders. The announcement of this range tended to overshadow the introduction of the DH 825, a smaller 8.25-litre power unit, also on view at the 1968 Amsterdam Show, but only in prototype form. It developed 156 bhp at 2,400 rpm.

This is a book about DAF's truck-making activities and the company's venture into car manufacture is well documented. Nevertheless, it is appropriate to cover something of this development because DAF's small car was also available as a light van. The car was launched at the Amsterdam Show of 1958, after three years of study and development, and by September 1964, the 100,000th DAF car had left the production line. As recorded earlier, it had an impact on DAF's truck-making activities, for space was needed for engine production for the car, and this led to the erection of the Oeval cab-making plant, leaving space at Eindhoven.

Like the car from which they were developed, the delivery van and pick-up versions had a DAF clutch and the Variomatic infinitely variable belt-drive automatic transmission. Rated for a payload of 0.35 tonnes (about 7 cwt) within a gross weight of 1.1 tonnes (22 cwt), plus the driver, this little delivery vehicle had the same 746cc twin-cylinder, horizontally opposed air-cooled engine as fitted to the car from 1962, which delivered a modest 32 bhp (SAE),

A tractor-unit version of the 2600-series model coupled to a DAF Eurotrailer. This had the cab which was introduced in 1964 and was amongst the European trendsetters in improving working conditions for the driver.

A modified radiator grille and front-end with headlamps recessed into the front bumper distinguished the 2000 series in the 1960s, when the DAF 11.6-litre engine was adopted. This is a 4 × 4 tipper version.

A 1960s refrigerated vehicle based on the popular 2000-series chassis, which took DAF through the decade.

which did not give it much help, I remember, on hill starts if the gradient was steep and the vehicle fully loaded. It was, however, an economical little vehicle for town delivery duties, consuming around 35 mpg on this class of work — a good 10 mpg better than most competitors, and it was surprising, perhaps, that because of this feature alone it did not meet with greater success.

One of the most intriguing versions of the DAF van was that produced in Sweden by the Kalmar concern, which developed a mail van for the Post Office using the same engine and Variomatic transmission system. Another development, as previously mentioned in the chapter on military vehicles, was the Pony, a lightweight 4 × 4 cross-country vehicle which also used DAF car components.

Then there was an American company, the Arkansas Louisiana Gas Company, which ordered power and transmission components for 100 ¼-ton pick-up trucks, which that concern built to its own special requirements. The company took this step because the other types of small vehicle it had used previously were found to have restrictive limitations and drivers did not like having to change gear so frequently. The series it designed had chassis frames on which were mounted different types of body, and this interesting exercise was indicative of the tremendous interest in this unusual but versatile concept at that time.

There was yet another use to which these DAF car components was put, and from the commercial vehicle operator's viewpoint it was probably the most interesting. DAF built a baby artic tractor unit version of the Pony, which, when coupled to a small semi-trailer, gave a payload of 1,600 kg. There was also a drawbar trailer version, which gave a payload of 750 kg on the two-axled hauling vehicle and about 1,100 kg on the two-axled trailer.

The two models were offered in a variety of forms including an open-cab version with or without body, a canvas cab-covered model without doors and an enclosed cab with doors. However, although exciting from the engineering viewpoint, the commercial vehicles derived from the car components were not really as robust as was necessary to cope with the jobs for which people bought them, and they were to disappear in the 1970s.

At the end of the 1960s, however, DAF had cause to be satisfied with most of its products. In 10 years the company had come a long way. It had no less than 13 different series of vehicles and 69 model ranges. Moreover, each model was offered in a number of different versions through the variations in wheelbase, gearbox and rear-axle ratios provided. In the 10-year span the company had developed its own engine range without producing a 'lemon'. It was now a question of consolidating on this success in the decade to come.

The best sellers in the 1960s — the TE 2600 DKA

Type:	TE 2600 DKA Series 4 × 2 articulated vehicle tractor unit for operation at 36-42 tons gross combination weight.
Engine:	DKA 1160, 11.6-litre six-cylinder, in-line diesel producing a maximum power of 250 bhp at 2,200 rpm (SAE) and a maximum torque of 597 lb ft at 1,300 rpm.
Gearbox:	ZF six-speed constant-mesh.
Wheelbases:	3.1 and 3.6 m.
Front axle:	Capacity 6.3 tonnes.
Rear axle:	DAF hub-reduction, capacity 13 tonnes, ratio 6.08:1, 6.84:1 or 7.93:1. Two-speed (8.94 or 6.84:1 ratios) and 7.93 and 6.08:1 self-locking differentials optionally available.
Brakes:	Dual-circuit air.
Cab:	Fixed forward-control in standard and sleeper form.

Chapter 5

Vehicles of the 1970s

DAF's model range which took the company into the 1970s obviously included some models which were intended primarily for sale in the Netherlands, but most of them were designed for DAF's complete market; it was a Eurodesign concept.

The first show of the 1970s was at Geneva in January of that year, which pre-empted the Amsterdam Show a month later by putting on public show for the first time DAF's new 13-to-36 metric tonne cruiserweight range, consisting of the F 1600, 1800, 2000 and 2200 to supersede the old DAF 1600, 1900 and 2200 series. DAF's bonneted equivalents were also phased-out at this time.

The series, which has turned out to be one of the most important ever for DAF, was distinguished by an entirely new flat-fronted, forward-control tilt cab, the tilting mechanism of which was impressive. By operating a release lever behind the seats and releasing an external catch it was possible for one man to tilt the cab forward through an angle of 60 degrees.

There were any number of other design changes which made this series totally different from that which it replaced. Pressed-steel cross-members were rivetted to the chassis frame instead of being welded, longer front and rear springs were fitted, with torsion bars added on tipper versions to check roll, and there was a 14.5-tonne gvw 4 × 4 chassis. The engines fitted ranged from DAF's DF615 diesel in two turbocharged forms, the DTD and DT615, producing in one instance 137 bhp (DIN) and in the other 153 bhp, both at 2,400 rpm, to the DH 825 with oil-cooler fitted in the heaviest models. For tipper and other designs requiring a power take-off, a horizontally disposed gearbox, which could be either constant-mesh or synchromesh, became available.

Engines and their power outputs, noise and emission levels were to be critical topics for manufacturers in the 1970s. A significant development took place on January 1, 1972, West Germany introduced a minimum power-to-weight ratio law for trucks of 8 bhp/ton. Recognizing that its top-end models had to meet this requirement, DAF introduced its DKB 1160, 11.6-litre engine rated at exactly 304 bhp (DIN), the minimum capacity needed to qualify for operation at 38 tonnes gross combination weight. This was unveiled at the Geneva Motor Show that month where versions of the DAF 2500 series artic tractor unit and drawbar trailer-hauling models, strengthened to take the increased performance, were also shown. In these applications, the engine had to be tilted to one side of the chassis to accommodate the KKK-Schwitzer blower within the non-tilt cab which was retained on these models.

Although DAF by this time was concentrating on its heavy and medium-heavy ranges, it did not ignore the light-medium market, and at Amsterdam the next month (February 1972) a new range of chassis for town delivery work in the 7-to-8-tonne payload class was introduced. This was the new 1200 and 1400 series, a range particularly intended for congested in-town and other short-distance operations. Heavier and

DAF's sturdy DKS 1160 six-cylinder turbocharged and after-cooled 11.6-litre engine in its 1973 form, when it produced a maximum power of 340 bhp (SAE) or 320 bhp (DIN) at 2,200 rpm.

more expensive than Bedford or Ford equivalents, they nevertheless were intended as 'premium' rivals to those makes, the specification being aimed to give them a longer working life at high annual mileages.

The tilt cab fitted was the same as that used on the 1970 introductions, but was 8 in narrower. Two different widths were allowed for in the original design so that DAF was able to omit a central strip from the front, rear and roof pressings to produce a cab only 6 ft wide overall, while a flat floor ahead of three seats gave unimpeded cross-cab access. On the 1200 models, 16-in wheels were fitted to give a chassis top height with the vehicle laden of only 31 in.

Undoubtedly one of the biggest merits for DAF was the new tilt cab introduced in 1969. In retrospect, it can be seen as a landmark in cab design because it successfully introduced the modular cab concept; one basic design fulfilled all the needs of the DAF range. This was feasible through the designers evisaging, right from the outset, that there would be a need for short versions, long versions, narrow ones, tall ones and short ones. As a result it was intended that inserts be incorporated in some and left out in others and a full set of pressings was developed to take account of this. Such a method of construction is now, of course, common practice, but it wasn't then.

As already indicated, DAF entered the 1970s with the most comprehensive range of power units it had ever had, so the company was in a position to offer an increasing number of derivatives from its basic chassis range. This was evident in the 1970 Geneva Show introductions, but the most significant development on this score was the introduction in 1973 of the F 2800 series.

Designed for heavy long-distance haulage, a sector of transport which DAF saw at the time as expanding at an increasingly rapid pace through European unification (the Common Market was expanding from six to nine countries at this time), the F 2800 series specification had, through the flexibility of its power unit production, a wide range of options to enable each vehicle to be tailored to its intended job. The series comprised truck, tipper and tractor chassis with four different engines with outputs ranging from 230 bhp to 320 bhp (DIN). There were two-axle and three-axle

models, the latter with single-drive or double-drive tandem axles, according to requirements.

The tilt cab had a tilting angle of 70 degrees to make the engine easily accessible from all sides, but daily oil and water checks could be made through the grille at the front. Much importance was attached to unrestricted vision in all directions, with the result that the cab had a large area of glass, three windscreen wipers, generously dimensioned mirrors and four headlamps. Two cab options were offered, a long cab with a sleeping compartment and a short cab without sleeping accommodation.

The power unit choice — all based on the DAF 11.6-litre diesel — resulted in power ratings of 230, 260, 290 and

An earlier DKT 1160 engine, dating from 1971, when the maximum power output of the direct-injection diesel was 310 bhp (SAE) or 290 bhp (DIN) at 2,200 rpm.

An F 2800-series four-wheeler with canvas tilt body hauling a three-axled drawbar trailer at 38 tonnes gross train weight.

13-tonne rear axle and with a 16-tonne or 20-tonne tandem axle, illustrating the point made earlier about DAF's increasing flexibility to meet the needs of markets outside the Netherlands.

One of the most interesting developments involving DAF in the early-1970s was the company's role in the Club of Four. As indicated in the chapter on corporate development, DAF was one of the companies — along with Magirus Deutz, Saviem and Volvo — in what was officially termed the European Truck Design programme. The four entered into an agreement in April 1972 jointly to develop and test components for a light truck range from 6 to 12 tonnes gross vehicle weight. These were the 500, 700, 900 and 1100 series, offered with a variety of engines, including a Perkins four-cylinder unit in the lightest versions, the 500 and 700, and the

320 bhp (DIN). Except for the lightest version, all these engines were turbocharged and the heaviest one also had cooling of the air inducted for combustion (intercooling). The 230 bhp and 260 bhp engines were coupled to a six-speed ZF AK690 gearbox supplemented as required by a splitter box, giving a total of 12 speeds. A 13-speed Fuller RTO 9513 gearbox was used with the two heavier engines, this being a twin-countershaft unit with constant-mesh gears, the lowest ratio being a crawler.

A new DAF 13-tonne rear axle with hub-reduction was introduced for this DAF truck series and hydraulic power steering was, of course, standard. These 2800s were also DAF's first models to fit dual-circuit air brakes meeting the EEC design standards. The suspension consisted of long, smooth springs on the rigid models, supplemented wherever necessary by shock absorbers and stabilizers, although tractor units for articulated-vehicle work had parabolic-type springs. The series was offered with the choice of either a 10-tonne or

The designation F 241 was given to the tilt cab shown here in its standard form fitted to an F 2800-series chassis in the early-1970s.

DAF 475 and 575 power units in 900 and 1100 series.

They were high-specification designs, produced in very limited quantities. DAF has never seemed to be very enthusiastic about getting heavily involved in this weight class of vehicle. Club of Four membership did mean, however, that DAF benefitted from common development of key components like the Club of Four cab, which in the DAF version is the F 200 unit.

Perhaps the biggest bonus for DAF from this co-operation was not apparent until well into the decade, not until 1977 in fact, when two new series — the F 1300 and F 1500 — were added. When DAF announced them, it was pointed out that the 1200 and 1300 series, which the newcomers displaced, did

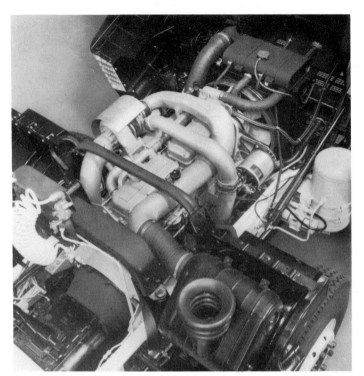

Excellent engine access is afforded by the F 241 cab of the F 2800 series when it is at its maximum tilt angle, as shown here.

The sleeper version of the F 241 cab on the F 2800 series showing the instrumentation and the high quality of the interior fittings.

not represent a logical continuation from the design angle of existing models (they were scaled-down versions of the 1600 series). The 1300 and 1500 series provided a more logical projection of the 500 to 1100 series into heavier weight categories.

Intended for medium-distance distribution, the 1300 and 1500 were introduced to carry a wide variety of loads, which meant a considerable variety in the nature of the goods carried and therefore variety in bodies and body lengths. The cab was the main difference from the previous designs, being the F 200 cab used for the 500 to 1100 series. A low step ahead of the front axle and a wide-opening door afforded easy access. Good interior cab access and an excellent view in all

A cutaway DAF 2699 rear axle showing the hub-mounted reduction gears and the generous brake lining area offered.

directions were other characteristics. The 1300 series had a gross vehicle weight of 11.8 tonnes, giving a gross carrying capacity of 7.8 to 7.9 tonnes, depending on the version. The 1500 series had a gross vehicle weight of 14 tonnes and a gross carrying capacity of 9.8 to 10 tonnes. Both were offered in four wheelbase-length variations. The DAF DF 615 and DT 615 engines, rated at 115 bhp and 153 bhp, were the respective power units, both achieving these outputs at 2,600 rpm. A five-speed ZF synchromesh gearbox was fitted in each instance.

Turning again to the cruiserweights, once the 2800 series had been introduced to follow the 2200, it was realized that there was a gap in the range, especially in terms of tractor units. The 2300 was evolved as the answer to the problem. Making its debut late in 1976, it was not surprising that the F 2300 series made use of a large number of components from these two other series. There was a 2300 and a 2305 version, the first, built for operation at 16 tonnes gross, being fitted with a 10-tonne rear axle and the latter a 13-tonne unit for operation at 19 tonnes.

As indicated, the tractors were the key models. These were available with the standard cab, developed from the 2200-series cab, or a slightly longer two-berth sleeper cab necessitating a longer wheelbase to enable the best possible tractor/semi-trailer combination to be achieved in all circumstances, but keeping within legal limits. With the standard cab, the 2300 was offered with wheelbases of 2.85 m and 3.25 m; wheelbase of the 2305 was 2.85 m. In contrast, in sleeper cab form, wheelbases of 3.25 m and 3.65 m were available for the 2300 series, with a wheelbase of 3.25 m for the 2305 version.

The turbocharged and charge-cooled version of DAF's six-cylinder, in-line, 8.25-litre DHU 825 diesel engine provided the power for the new range. In adopting turbocharging with charge-cooling DAF took advantage of its development work on the 320 bhp (DIN) version of its 11.6-litre engine. The DHU 825 in this form developed 230 bhp (DIN) at 2,400 rpm and was coupled to a ZF six-speed or nine-speed gearbox.

Once the 2300 series had been launched, the remaining part of the 1970s constituted a period of consolidation for DAF. As the company explained at the time, the standardization of the medium-heavy part of the truck range, which began with the introduction of the FT 2300 DHU, was continued, several new models being added to the 2300 series during the

Generous non-slip steps for the driver and his mate and an equally generous provision of window area reflect the attention to driver requirements in the F 241 cab.

DAF's designation for this cab on the F 1500 series was F 200. A tilt cab design, it incorporated many pressings common with the F 241 cab.

Frankfurt Show of 1977, together with the first model in the 2100 series, a tractor chassis. After that the 2100 and 2300 were rounded-off, to complete the standardization of this part of the DAF range. Standardization, it was explained, implied frequent use of the same well-tried components in different vehicles.

In the 2300 series, for example, single-drive tandem-axle models were added and, with the introduction of a turbocharged and charge-cooled 230 bhp engine, this meant there was a choice of three 8.25-litre engines (the other two being a naturally aspirated 163 bhp unit and a turbocharged 204 bhp version) for all models in this series, namely, two-axle trucks and tractors and three-axle vehicles with 6 × 2

and 6 × 4 configuration.

As far as the 2100 series was concerned, 4 × 2 and 6 × 2 truck models joined the tractor units already in production. Intended for the medium-heavy part of the market, these models superseded the corresponding models in the 2000 series. Apart from the advantages conferred by standardization, they provided more possibilities than the 2000-series models. With gross vehicle weights of 16 tonnes for the FA 2100 series and 17.5 tonnes for the 2105 series, they had higher payloads and increased power because the DHR 825, 204 bhp (DIN) engine was introduced in addition to the DH 825 unit of 163 bhp.

These developments reflected once again DAF's efforts to

standardize various parts of its range. One disadvantage found, however, was that vehicles with greatly differing technical specifications strongly resembled each other. To solve this problem, model designations were accordingly introduced on all DAF cabs, the model number (1100, 2300, 2800 and so on) being shown on every vehicle. If a vehicle was fitted with a turbocharged engine, the word 'Turbo' was added to the number. If the engine was charge-cooled 'Intercooling' was added. The 2800 DKS had to bear the designation '2800-Turbo-Intercooling', the 1500 DT '1500-Turbo' and the 2100 DH '2100' without any additions.

In the mid-1970s, DAF's trailer production was still very much part of its production mix and, as with heavy-duty artic tractor-unit production, it laid emphasis on designs for international haulage. These Eurotrailers, as they were called, stemmed from designs of the 1960s. They proved very popular and culminated in a model, introduced in 1975, which incorporated a host of new features. It was a self-supporting box-type van, with one-piece roof and built completely of aluminium panels and sections attached to each other without rivets. It could be built to a variety of carrying capacities and could be fitted with single-axle running gear for a gross weight of 26 or 32 tonnes or with tri-axle running gear for a gross weight of 36 tonnes. It had a low vehicle weight for a box-type van. For instance, a complete Eurotrailer with a 20-tonne tandem axle weighed 5,160 kg, to give a gross carrying capacity of 26,840 kg, although obviously the weight of the floor and any internal panelling

DAF's single-spine-chassis distribution vehicle, shown here carrying a mixture of drinks in barrels and bottles on pallets; note the ultra-low loading height afforded.

The popular 'in between' model of the 1970s was the F 2300 series, shown here in 6 × 4 form.

An internal view of the DAF F 220 short-version tilt cab fitted to the DAF FT 2100 tractor unit introduced in 1977.

had to be deducted from this.

This range was introduced before some European countries raised their maximum articulated-vehicle length to 15.5 m so it was constructed primarily for a combination length not exceeding 15.0 m. Even then, the internal loading length of 12.23 m was a useful one. In countries in which a combination length of 15.5 m was permitted, the Eurotrailer could be given an additional bay on special application, making it 0.57 m longer and giving an internal length of 12.8 m. On all versions the internal width was 2.42 m, to facilitate the transport of pallets built to the internationally agreed standard. The total capacity of the standard-length Eurotrailer was more than 71 m³ and that of the extra-long version more than 74 m³. Trailer production ceased, of course, in 1979.

Apart from still being involved in trailer-making, DAF, at this time, still tended occasionally to move away from its regular production to manufacture models with relatively limited appeal. One such venture was into tractors for marshalling container semi-trailers in terminal yards and for roll-on, roll-off operation. Designated the TT 1301 DF and TT 1302 DF, these tractors differed from each other principally in respect of their gearbox and rear axle.

The 1301 model was the lighter version, mainly intended for marshalling work at ports, factories and transhipment centres and for ferry transport. It had a gross train weight capacity of 60 metric tons. The heavier 1302 model was designed for arduous roll-on, roll-off work. Rather ambitiously, it might be thought, account was taken of developments in container-handling, tending towards higher gross train weights, with the result that it had a gross train weight capability of 100-120 tonnes. Both were fitted with the DAF DF 615 diesel engine rated at 126 bhp (DIN), matched with Allison automatic transmissions, the MT 650 on the lighter version and the CRT 3331-3 on the heavier one.

An important new feature, compared with DAF's previous terminal tractors, was the one-man tilt cab with hydraulic tilting up to an angle of 54 degrees. An hydraulically lifted fifth-wheel coupling was fitted to make it easier to move semi-trailers to and fro, the coupling being raised by twin hydraulic rams to any height between 1.15 m and 2.05 m. The design permitted semi-trailers to be coupled-up automatically, and they were uncoupled pneumatically from the cab by remote-control. The hydraulic lifting device for the fifth-wheel coupling was likewise operated from the cab, enabling height adjustments to be made while on the move, as and when necessary.

Another example of DAF's willingness to cater for sectional needs came in 1978 when, at the Amsterdam Show, DAF introduced a single-spine chassis in which the normal chassis frame was replaced by a single member from about 0.85 m behind the cab. It added 100 kg to the chassis weight and was intended for operators in the bottled drinks trade, for operators carrying gas cylinders and plate glass, and other applications requiring plenty of space on each side of the

The single-spine F 2000-series chassis, introduced by DAF in 1977, was designed to permit a low loading height body to be fitted, with the body divided longitudinally over the spine.

A bodied version of the F 2000-series chassis showing a structure designed for carrying gas cylinders.

A 2000-series vehicle of 1970 fitted with a refuse collecting body.

chassis; it permitted a very low load deck on each side of the chassis, so simplyfying loading and unloading.

The show model was based on an F 2000 chassis, but similar conversions could be made of other chassis, such as the 2100 or 2300. The FM 2000, on which this first conversion was based, was given a longer wheelbase of 5.86 m, making it possible to fit superstructure with five 1.30 metres-long compartments to facilitate use with standard metric pallets. The air reservoirs, batteries and fuel tank were grouped together immediately behind the cab, brake lines and electrical wiring being routed under the central member.

The company had also become aware of the need to serve individual markets. Notably, in 1976, it presented the DAF FAD 2205 DU 30-tonnes GVW 8 × 4 tipper chassis at the request of its British company and primarily for the UK market. Designed around a light, strong frame with boxed

tipping cross-member as standard, this had the DAF 8.25-litre turbocharged engine, developing 216 bhp at 2,400 rpm and a torque of 528 lb ft at 1,800 rpm. There was also the F 2800 Supercontinental — referred to in detail in the chapter on DAF's British venture — which was also remarkably successful on the Continental mainland when shown at Amsterdam in 1976.

There were some 'oddball' things as well. At the 1971 Brussels Show there was a development which made the headlines all round the world. This, in fact, had almost nothing to do with DAF except that a DAF chassis was involved. I refer to the announcement by DAF's Eindhoven neighbour, the Philips electrical concern, of work on the development of the Stirling hot-gas external-combustion engine. Optimistically — and quite wrongly, as it has already turned out — Philips reckoned then that the Stirling engine would replace the diesel within 10 years. The four-cylinder, water-cooled engine was fitted in a DAF bus chassis, where it was designed to develop 200 bhp at 3,000 rpm. As indicated, DAF were not closely involved in this, but it certainly created a lot of interest at the time and gave a boost to the DAF name.

Air suspension was offered as an option increasingly in the 1970s, especially on the rear suspension of two and three-axle rigids and on tractor units. A special merit of this was that a special control valve made it possible for the vehicle to act as a pneumatic lifting device, enabling it to be run under, or out from under, a demountable body. A further important aspect of the option was that it gave a much smoother ride. This was of obvious benefit to a vehicle carrying delicate equipment, such as computers and breakable goods, including china and glass or volatile chemicals. Levelling valves kept the chassis frame, and consequently the vehicle platform, at a constant height irrespective of whether the vehicle was loaded or not.

In DAF's designs of the late-1970s, air suspension was fitted as an option to the rear axle and attached to the chassis frame with two special guide springs, instead of the normal

This was a 6 × 6 version of the F 2200 tipper chassis introduced in 1972. It had its cab and chassis mounted higher from the ground than standard versions to give greater mobility over rough ground.

The F 2000 and F 2200 series, introduced in 1970, had a tilt cab which set design standards for the 1970s. This particularly smart outfit had quite a few extras including special wheel trims.

The DAF FAS 2105 DHR was powered by the DAF DHR 8.25-litre six-cylinder turbocharged diesel engine rated at 202 bhp (BSAU 141A) with 494 lb ft of torque. The engine is coupled to a ZF AK 6-65 six-speed constant-mesh gearbox with a GV 80 two-speed splitter box.

Aerodynamic wind deflectors became a common sight on vehicles towards the end of the 1970s. This German-registered F 2300-series van and drawbar van trailer was photographed in 1979.

A 2100-series distribution vehicle being unloaded by a fork-lift truck. In this application the body is demountable, and once emptied a loaded body (such as the one on the right) is ready to be switched with the empty unit.

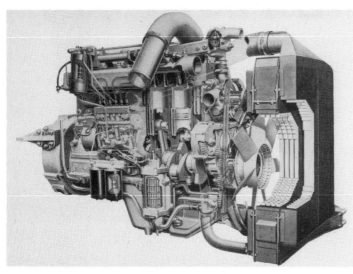

Above left, DAF's DHU 825 six-cylinder 8.25-litre diesel engine was the bedrock of success of its cruiserweight ranges. This version was fitted in the 2300 series in 1976 when it produced 230 bhp (DIN) at 2,400 rpm. Above, this DAF FA 2105 DH had the ZF S 6-65 six-speed gearbox — the first synchromesh unit to be offered as standard — and the 8.25-litre DAF DH engine producing 156 bhp and 372 lb ft of torque. Below left, the advanced F 220 tilt cab, seen here in its sleeper version, was a major selling point with the FT 2300 series. Below, the F 1300 and F 1500 DF series were introduced in 1978 for delivery duties.

This F 2300-series four-wheeler had the F 220 tilt cab when shown in this form to the industry in 1976.

rear springs. These two-leaf guide springs were mounted on pivots at the front in the original spring brackets, the other ends being shaped to fit in guide plates on the chassis frame to give sideways location to the axle. The lower spring leaves continued downwards and were linked by a cross-beam immediately behind the axle. The two air bellows were mounted on this beam. A separate air reservoir provided the air for the suspension system, so that it was thus independent of the braking system. In view of the fact that the suspension system itself had little internal friction, compared with normal leaf springs, double-acting shock absorbers were employed. A stabilizer was fitted to give good roll stability.

In technical terms, however, the most significant developments by DAF in the second half of the 1970s centred on environmental improvements and energy-saving. Of these, the most important was the announcement of the economy version of the DKS 1160 11.6-litre engine, featuring exhaust gas turbocharging and charge-cooling. The distinctive features of the economy version of the DKS engine were a maximum engine speed reduced to 1,800 rpm and a torque that increased considerably as the engine speed dropped. Whereas the earlier DKS 1160 engine delivered 856 lb ft of torque at 1,500 rpm, on the new economy version, designated the DKSE, torque at 1,800 rpm was 806 lb ft, but it rose as high as 929 lb ft when the engine speed dropped to 1,300 rpm.

DAF explained that the result of this operation — from the point of view of fuel consumption — was that it was only possible to use the most favourable part of the engine-speed range. The higher torque available greatly reduced the amount of gear-changing that was necessary. Moreover, the fuel consumption was affected less by the way in which the vehicle was driven than was in the case with the DKS engine.

Quite rightly, DAF is very proud of its engine development work. Its current engine development and test facilities are

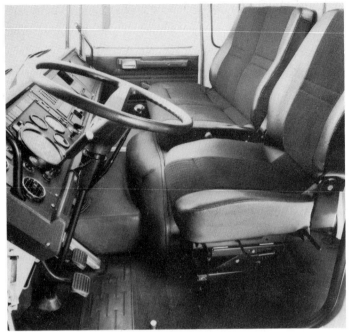

Cab comfort was always of special importance for DAF. This is the interior of the well-appointed cab of the F 1300/F 1500 series.

lower maximum engine speed gave the DAF engine designers more scope to improve the cylinder charge at lower engine speeds, so eliminating the restrictions on the choice of exhaust-gas turbocharger imposed by the higher maximum engine speeds that normally apply. Other plus points for the concept are less dirtiness from oil leaks, and engine wear is favourably influenced by the fact that the piston speed is relatively low, as are various inertia forces. A lower engine speed also means a lower noise level, for both the driver and the outside world. The lower engine speed is also likely to have a favourable effect on other components of the driveline and therefore upon repair bills (and downtime).

Basically, the DKS 1160 and the DKS 1160E engines as

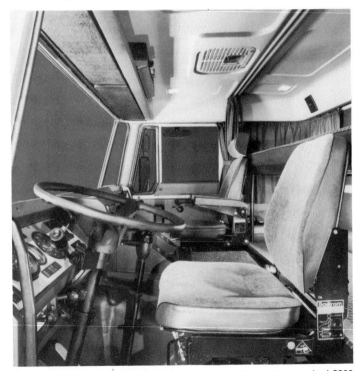

An interior shot of the F 241 tilt cab fitted on the 'second generation' 2800 series showing the high quality of the cab's finish and appointments.

regarded of particular significance at Eindhoven and it stresses the benefits obtained by combining turbocharging, charge-cooling, a limited maximum engine speed and a higher torque in one and the same engine as in the DKS 1160E. Forcing a greater quantity of air into the cylinder, DAF points out, enables the thermal efficiency of the engine to be improved. It also explains that the highest thermal efficiency is attained if an exhaust-gas turbocharger is used as it utilizes part of the energy present in the exhaust gases. Lower specific frictional losses (as compared with the naturally aspirated version) make for better mechanical efficiency.

Charge-cooling results in even more air being taken in, and, relatively speaking, in even less friction, again improving both thermal and mechanical efficiency. Moreover, charge-cooling lowers the temperature, reducing engine wear. The

F 1600 models appeared at the same time as the new 2000 series in 1970 and, as with this example, they featured the then new tilt cab.

A tanker outfit hauled by an F 2800/ F 2805 6 × 2 tractor fitted with lifting axle for use when running unladen.

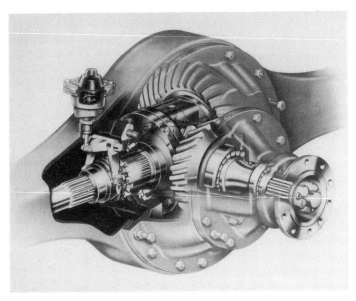

A cutaway drawing showing the installation and operation of the DAF lockable differential.

fitted to the 2800-series models were the same, both being 11.6-litre, six-cylinder, turbocharged and charge-cooled diesel engines. In addition to turbocharging and charge-cooling, both engines featured oil-cooling of piston crowns, oil/water heat exchangers, a thermal fan and twin thermostats. Beyond this, the DKSE engine was given a modified turbocharger, supplying more air at lower engine speed. It also had revised governor settings, and its introduction was quickly followed by the announcement of a second-generation 2800 series.

The revised 2800 was fitted with the ZF S 130 all-synchromesh gearbox (eight-speeds plus splitter with a double 'H' shift pattern) — a special selection for use in conjunction with the DKSE engine. The gearbox was matched with the DAF 2699 hub-reduction rear axle giving a total reduction

ratio of 4.49:1. A face-lifted cab with double-glazed rear and rear-side windows and an electrically operated window on the nearside also distinguished the improved range, and there were modified electrical and other detail features which were all introduced without a price increase.

DAF followed up the DKSE engine with the announcement of a device at the 1980 Amsterdam Show which it claimed could make a further substantial contribution to the achievement of better fuel consumption and give a longer life for turbocharged engines. Known as VISAR, the device — mounted in the cab of a truck — gives a permanent indication of fuel consumption and advises on gear-changing. Fuel consumption is read electronically, the engine load and the engine speed being recorded, thus making the specific fuel consumption known. By adding the vehicle speed, it is possible to calculate the fuel consumption in litres per 100 km (or mpg). With the VISAR system, the fuel consumption is indicated on a gauge which has not only figures, but also colour segments; 'green' means economical and 'red' the opposite.

A second function of VISAR — to advise on gear-changing — is also an interesting feature. If the vehicle is being driven with an engine-output/speed combination which could be improved — for example, if the engine power required is also available at a lower, more economical engine speed — the driver will be advised to change up by an indication on the instrument panel. If, on the other hand, the engine speed has dropped below the permissible level, he will be advised to change down.

The VISAR system also gives information relating to engine condition. This is done by measuring the engine charge pressure and indicating it on the VISAR instrument. If the charge pressure is lower than normal this may mean that the engine setting is incorrect, but it could also indicate an engine fault.

DAF has an impressive habit of monitoring what the market wants, and this, with its lively approach to technical development, seems likely to make the company an ever-increasing force in the commercial-vehicle world.

Cutaway of the DAF 2699 single-drive rear axle revealing the installation of the differential and the hub-reduction gears.

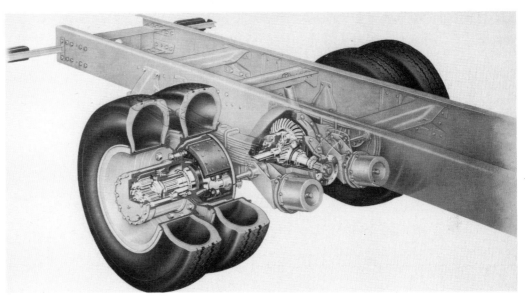

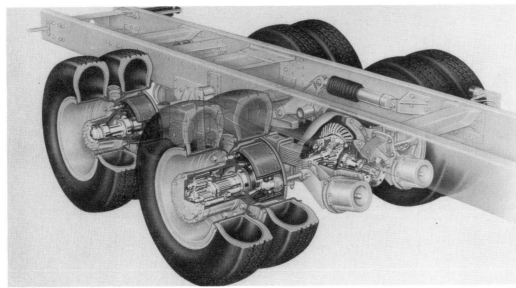

The 2699 was also offered with a trailing axle for heavier-duty applications.

An alternative transmission to the 2699 was this 2255 T tandem-drive installation, the detail layout of which can be seen clearly in this cutaway illustration.

Special vehicles have always formed part of DAF's portfolio; this is a relatively recent version of the company's special-purpose tractor unit for handling trailers on roll-on, roll-off ferries.

The best sellers in the 1970s — the F 2800*

Type:	F 2800 series, three models — FT 2800 DKTD 4 × 2, 42 tonnes gross combination weight tractor unit; FT DKS 4 × 2, 51 tonnes gross combination weight tractor unit; FTT 2805 DKS 6 × 4 51 tonnes gross combination weight tractor unit.	Wheelbases:	FT 2800 DKTD 4 × 2: 3.1 m. FT 2800 DKS 4 × 2: 3.1 m and 3.5 m. FTT 2805 DKS 6 × 4: 3.6 m.
		Front axles:	Capacity 6.5 tonnes.
Engines:	In the FT 2800 DKTD: the DAF DKTD 1160, 11.6-litre, six-cylinder diesel producing a maximum power of 252 bhp (BSAU 141a) and a maximum torque of 660 lb ft. In the FT DKS and the FTT 2805 DKS: the DKS 11.6-litre turbocharged and charged-cooled unit producing a maximum 307 bhp (BSAU 141a) and a maximum torque of 855 lb ft.	Rear axles:	FT 2800 DKTD 4 × 2: the DAF 2699 hub-reduction, ratio 5.53:1. Capacity 13 tonnes. FT 2800 DKS 4 × 2: the DAF 2699 hub-reduction, ratio 5.03:1. Capacity 13 tonnes. FTT 2805 DKS 6 × 4: the DAF 2255T, two-spring tandem-drive bogie with lockable inter-axle differential, ratio 5.72:1.
		Brakes:	Dual-circuit air (EEC system). Spring parking unit. Air-operated exhaust brake. Load sensing on rear axle.
Gearboxes:	In the FT 2800 DKTD: the ZF AK 6-90 six-speed constant-mesh unit with GV-90 two-speed splitter. In the FT 2800 DKS and the FTT 2805 DKS: the Fuller RTO 9513, 13-speed constant-mesh unit.	Cab:	Tilt unit in standard and sleeper form.

*Typical late-1970s specification.

The best sellers in the 1970s — the FT 2300*

Type:	FT 2300 DHU 4 × 2, 36 tonnes gross combination weight tractor unit.	Rear axles:	DAF 2699 hub-reduction, ratio 5.53:1. Capacity 19.5 tonnes or 16.27 tonnes.
Engine:	DHU 825 8.25-litre six-cylinder turbocharged, charge-cooled diesel engine, producing a maximum 230 bhp and 572 lb ft of torque.	Brakes:	Dual-circuit air (EEC system). Spring parking unit. Air-operated exhaust brake. Load sensing on rear axle.
Gearbox:	ZF 5K nine-speed constant-mesh.	Cab:	F220 type, standard and sleeper versions.
Overall length:	5.23 m and 5.63 m.		
Wheelbase:	2.85 m and 3.25 m.		
Front axles:	Capacity 6.5 or 6.1 tonnes.		

*Typical late-1970s specification.

Chapter 6

DAF as an exporter

To succeed as a vehicle manufacturer it is accepted that you have to have a strong home market. DAF adopted this principle, one suspects, because it had at the time no real alternative, establishing first a strong base within the frontiers of the Netherlands, but spilling over into a second 'home' market formed by the Benelux countries.

It was realized from the start that Belgium would be almost as important as a sales territory for DAF as the Netherlands, and it was for this reason that DAF Belgie NV was the first company established beyond the Dutch border. In fact, DAF had a company there as early as 1934 as far as trailers and semi-trailers were concerned. The present Belgian company, however, dates from 1950, a fact which underlines DAF's view, right from the start of its activities as a powered-vehicle manufacturer, that its principal sales territories should be the Benelux countries.

DAF was not particularly export-minded in the 1950s, or even the early-1960s. The company occasionally sold vehicles outside the Benelux countries, but there was no strong effort to do so, and DAF did not establish any organization other than the Belgian one outside the Netherlands until DAF France SA was formed in 1961. As indicated elsewhere, this coincided with the uplift in the Dutch heavy vehicle weight limits, bringing them much more into line with those of France, save for the fact that France had higher axle weight limits than the Netherlands of 13 tonnes on a single axle and a maximum of 20 tonnes on a bogie. DAF was already having

to build to these weights because they had been adopted in Belgium and were thus a feature of its 'home' market. The Belgian and French markets were catered for by the optional offer of heavier axles in DAF's top-of-the-range models.

Although this French move can be seen as a logical extension of DAF's home market, it occurred at a time when international haulage operations were increasing rapidly in Europe. Priority, therefore, was given to providing proper back-up for such activities, and it seemed logical that this should centre on a French location.

It was in 1964 that DAF really started to tackle the question of its sales and service network in Europe. Measures taken included the establishment of its European headquarters at Survilliers, on the Paris-Brussels motorway, which was then under construction, and offices and workshops at Hamburg, Frankfurt and Munich, in addition to the existing headquarters in Dusseldorf. The first moves were also made to establish a branch in Milan.

These facilities formed part of an overall plan to set up a chain of sales-service points on the main international road transport routes. This was to become DAF's International Truck Service (ITS) in 1969, which has since been built up to become one of, if not the most extensive heavy-vehicle service and repair networks in Europe. A measure of its success is that it handled no less than 7,500 emergencies in 1979 and got 98 per cent of the vehicles involved back on the road within 24 hours.

Exports were not big business for DAF in the 1950s and 1960s with the exception of Belgium and France. However, occasionally there were orders from further afield, as, for example, for this car transporter outfit, above, seen operating in Argentina, and this truck, right, engaged on tricky timber-loading duties in West Africa.

If DAF had any real export strategy at all in the 1960s it was to increase sales in the Common Market territories, the Netherlands of course, being one of the original six members of the European Economic Community.

A DAF company was set up in West Germany in the 1960s but, in the beginning, it was concerned more with cars than trucks. This mixture of cars being tied up with trucks was not a success in export terms, as DAF found in Britain in particular. There is little doubt that had the car and truck activities remained in the hands of the DAF car organization in Britain, as they were in the early-1970s, DAF would never have been anything like as successful in the truck field.

In fact both the German and British truck-importing companies were formed in 1973, DAF Nutzfahrzeuge

With the development of its 2800 series DAF introduced this 6 × 4 version for the arduous conditions encountered in Africa and the Middle East. Features include cab air-conditioning, sun visor and sun shield for the top of the cab.

The F 2800 series found increasing acceptance in Germany for lorry and drawbar trailer hauling, as with this locally registered 1975 outfit.

Deutschland GmbH at Langenfeld, and DAF Trucks (GB) Ltd at Marlow. The German company established a subisidiary in Austria in the same year — split off from the cars — called DAF Nutzfahrzeuge-Handelsgesellschaft GmbH, located at Wiener Neudorf. Later, in 1975, this became a company in its own right, with direct links with Eindhoven, the West German link then being severed.

The establishment of the German and British companies were landmarks for DAF in that they reflected management recognition of the need to expand outside the company's traditional sales territories. Just how dependent DAF was on the Benelux markets and France is revealed by the 1971 statistics. In that year, out of 8,300 commercial vehicles produced, no less than 53 per cent were sold in the Netherlands and 25 per cent in Belgium and France. A total of 78 per cent of all sales in 'home' territories makes a company vulnerable in times of market depression. DAF realized this and acted in time following a recommendation to this effect by the international firm of management consultants mentioned in Chapter 2.

DAF's key location in France is positioned strategically at Survilliers, on the main motor routes.

Of the remaining 22 per cent of production in 1971, most of the vehicles were sold in other European countries, which was very much in line with its EEC export sales policy. It is also relevant that, by this time, the company had over 300 service points in Europe and was extending its network increasingly in Eastern Europe and the Middle East.

Recognition of the need to expand exports was also reflected in the 1972 deal with International Harvester, even though it failed to work out in practice. DAF said at the time that the agreement stemmed from two differing, yet complementary requirements. DAF needed to move into markets in which to sell its products, while International Harvester had a well-organized sales network in many parts of the world, but had several gaps in its range. As part of the agreement, therefore, International Harvester was to market DAF commercial vehicles alongside its own products through its extensive dealer network in Africa, Asia, Australia and the United States.

In the event, of course, this just did not happen, although there were one or two half-hearted attempts, including the appearance of the bonneted IH Paystar on the DAF stand at the next Amsterdam Show and the export through IH of some DAFs to the USA. Fortunately for DAF, its other export moves met with a greater degree of success; as will be indicated in the next chapter its success in the UK was outstanding.

One of DAF's most modern overseas locations is its Austrian service and parts centre at Wiener Neudorf.

Langenfeld is the location of DAF's headquarters in Germany.

The company did not do badly in other places, either. DAF has always sold well in France, where it has been the No. 2 heavy vehicle importer for some years. It also did well in the tough German market, whilst its record in Italy, where DAF Trucks Italia SpA was established at Cusago in 1974, was highly satisfactory when the company really started selling in 1978. Before this date it had only provided service facilities.

There seems little doubt that DAF has gained the measure of success that it has by adopting a policy of establishing its own companies in European territories rather than selling through importers. In some places, however, importers have been used — in Switzerland, for example — but in 1978 DAF decided to set up its own company there as well, and formed DAF Schweiz AG in Zurich.

Switzerland is a special market. It has a gross-weight limit for trucks of 28 tonnes and a maximum width on roads other than motor routes of 2.3 metres. This resulted in DAF announcing a purpose-built 2.3 metres wide maximum-capacity vehicle for the Swiss market at the Geneva Truck & Bus Show in January 1980. The DAF FA 2805 DKS, as it is termed, is 2.3 m wide, has a modified 2300-series cab and an 11.6-litre engine producing 310 bhp (DIN/EEC).

The design particularly reflects DAF's versatility in cab construction in that it has been able to reduce the width without incurring undue cost as a result of the modular production concept already described. This flexibility in vehicle production is particularly apparent in the models developed for the UK market which are dealt with in the next chapter. A further example is represented by the 44-tonner developed for the Italian market in the late-1970s.

The decision to set up a DAF-owned company in Switzerland, however, was one of the first moves marking the introduction of a total marketing and export strategy by DAF. There have been quite a few moves since and a lot more are planned. For instance, as 1979 drew to a close, DAF announced that preparations were well under way for the export of commercial vehicles to Sweden through its importer, DAF Lastbilar of Stockholm. This concern started up on January 1, 1980, operating through DAF's Nordic office in Gothenburg. DAF's F 2800 series, modified to meet the legal requirements in Sweden, was the vehicle chosen for

NV DAF Belgie's modern premises at Artselaar.

the assault on this market. It met with early success, sales topping the 100 mark in the first three months of 1980.

Elsewhere in Europe, DAF's remaining activities centred on Spain and Portugal. In the case of Spain, DAF had a trailer plant operating as DAF SAE, in Madrid, for many years, but this was shut down at the end of 1978 as part of DAF's planned phasing-out of its trailer-making activities.

The military department of DAF Trucks, in close co-operation with DAF SAE in Madrid, liaised over a lengthy period with ENASA (Pegaso) on DAF military-vehicle designs, which the Spanish company produced under licence. In Portugal, some DAF vehicles are assembled locally from ckd kits by Proval, in Lisbon. DAF also makes quite a few direct sales to Greece, Norway and Denmark.

Outside the European sphere, DAF has set its sights particularly on the Middle East and Africa. Here, the most significant move has been the setting-up of regional sales offices in Dubai and Abidjan and the appointment of Saudi Arabian Truck Agencies (SATA) as the DAF importer for

This narrow-cab (2.3 m wide) model in its 2100 series (an FA 2105 DHR) was built specifically for the Swiss market. It fits the DAF 8.25-litre 204 bhp (DIN) six-cylinder turbocharged diesel engine and ZF 12-speed synchromesh gearbox. Payload is up to around 10½ tonnes.

Saudi Arabia. SATA, a company formed early in 1980, is controlled and staffed by DAF-trained personnel. The agreement was signed in Jeddah in January of that year by Mr Piet van Doorne, on behalf of DAF, and HRH Prince Bander Bin Abdul-Aziz, owner of Saudi Arabian Truck Agencies, which has its headquarters in Jeddah.

Priority actions of SATA are to establish sales, service and parts outlets in the principal commercial centres of Jeddah, Riyadh and Dammam. Offices were opened in January 1980, and modern workshop complexes were built in Jeddah and Dammam. A service point with a comprehensive spares stock exists at Riyadh, but this was scheduled to be upgraded in 1981 to a newly constructed workshop and parts complex. The DAF truck models most in demand in this area are the top of the range F 2805 series, available as a tractor unit, heavy-duty tipper, general cargo truck and tanker.

Apart from the Middle East, DAF also has an interest in Accra, Ghana, where an assembly operation was started by Autoparts Ltd, in 1978. The assembly operation, which consists of the supply from the Netherlands of components and sub-assemblies for the building of the complete vehicle in Accra, has been confined to DAF's FA 1600 truck and FT 2805 tractor models.

All parts and sub-assemblies are supplied through DAF's Accra importers, Standard Motors Industry Ltd. Greater Ghanaian involvement in production is planned as the operation settles down, reflecting the fact that West African markets are slowly closing to the import of complete vehicles. Nigeria has been the scene of an important operation centred on Lagos, and the Ivory Coast is yet another territory which is proving a useful export market. Kenya placed orders with the company for over 100 vehicles in 1979.

Built for a payload of up to 9 tonnes, this Swiss-registered FA 1600 DT complies with Switzerland's 2.3 m width limit applied on specified roads. The DAF 6.15-litre turbocharged engine is matched in this application by a 10-speed ZF gearbox and a two-speed back axle.

Among the relatively small number of vehicles exported in the 1950s was this South African 40-series unit with van body operated by Excelsior Bakeries.

A very significant export development was made public in July 1980. It was the surprise announcement that the giant Hungarian truck manufacturer RABA was to buy DAF truck cabs and chassis side-members. Hitherto it had always fitted MAN units under an agreement which is due to come to an end in 1982.

How was DAF placed in its export markets as the company entered the 1980s? Mr Piet van Doorne gave the answers at a pre-Amsterdam Show 1980 press conference in Eindhoven and they are worth quoting as they provide a clear picture of the state of the market for DAF in export terms and its plans for the future.

In 1979, DAF's market share in the Netherlands increased from 34 to 36 per cent in a rather large market of around 12,000 units in the category above 9 tonnes, and parts sales went up by 20 per cent.

The Belgian market expanded by 4 per cent, more or less in step with the recovery in the transport sector and the economy in general. DAF's share in the category above 7.5 tonnes was around 17 per cent, against 15.5 per cent in 1978. DAF

Belgium reached first place in the league of suppliers of tractive units.

DAF France had a good year, in fact a record one. The market share (in its category) rose from 3.8 to 5 per cent. Much attention was devoted to improving the quality of the dealer organization. Weak dealers were replaced, and new dealers were appointed at places where there had been no sales-and-service centres until then. The French DAF organization now operates with 44 dealers and three branches of its own.

A larger number of deliveries and a higher market share than in 1978 were also reported from Austria, where the financial results were more favourable than expected. In order to improve service to customers in the Vienna area, it had been decided to extend the workshop facilities at DAF's Wiener Neudorf HQ.

Turning to Switzerland, Mr van Doorne said that 1979 was the first year in which DAF had operated with a subsidiary of its own in that country. Although this was a very difficult market, DAF had managed to sell about 50 vehicles, a market

Built for the Swiss market, the DAF FAT 2805 DKS is available in 2.3 m and 2.5 m wide versions. The engine is the 11.6-litre turbocharged unit producing 310 bhp, matched with the Fuller RTO 9513 13-speed gearbox.

France and Belgium are catered for by specifications to suit their markets. This is an F 2800/2805-series 6 × 4 tractor unit built for heavy-duty work of the type illustrated.

share of 1.7 per cent. An important fact in this connection was that the 2100, 2300 and 2800 series were now available with a width of 2.30 m with the narrow version of the 2800 series employing a suitably modified F 220 cab.

In Italy, DAF's subsidiary had been energetically engaged in expanding its dealer organization, 12 new dealers having been appointed. A most important event was the introduction of the 2800 with the DKSI engine, developed specially for Italy. This model was designed for a gross combination weight of 44 tonnes, as was customary in Italy, and to meet the Italian requirement of 8 bhp per tonne. As a result of the strengthening of the organization and the sales range, chassis deliveries were three times as high as in 1978.

The United Kingdom was, he said, still DAF's best foreign market. Despite increasing competition from other importers, the company's market share rose from 3.7 to 4 per cent.

The Export Division, which he explained, looked after sales to non-EEC countries, was not able to operate in the most favourable circumstances in 1979 and political disturbances and economic problems clearly had an adverse effect on sales

A 1979/80 2300-series tractor unit hauling a German beer tanker fitted with tri-axle running gear.

in a number of overseas export markets. Furthermore, partly as a result of excess production in Europe, DAF had encountered keen competition. In spite of this, DAF's sales and deliveries in 1979 showed a better picture than in 1978, and the regional offices opened in Abidjan, Dubai and Gothenburg had proved their worth in maintaining contact with local importers and markets in their areas and promoting interest in DAF.

After referring to the establishment of Svenska DAF Lastbilar in Sweden, he went on to say that the considerable improvements which the company's importers in Norway, Greece, Reunion and Egypt had made to their facilities were of much significance to DAF's operations in these markets. Several of the DAF importers were very active in the bus field, while those in Morocco and Greece also built bus bodies and in both these countries a considerable number of buses had been sold.

Mr van Doorne concluded by saying that exports to countries outside Europe would probably remain difficult for the time being, compared with European sales, but DAF was convinced that there were good possibilities in the longer term. For instance, a slight economic recovery was occurring in West Africa, whilst due, amongst other things, to the efforts of the company's regional office at Abidjan, increasing interest was being shown there in DAF products.

The announcement of its bonneted N 2800 and export forward-control 2100 and 2300 series in November 1980 reflected DAF's increasing sales efforts in the Middle East and Africa through its divisional export offices at Dubai. Their announcement followed extensive market research and prototype testing in these areas.

The N 2800 is available as a 6 × 4 rigid and a 6 × 4 tractor unit for articulated-vehicle use, the 6 × 4 having a designed gross weight of 31.5 tonnes, but with substantial overloading capability, and the tractor units for 42 tonnes and 56 tonnes gross combinations weight, according to the engine fitted. The rigid is made in two wheelbase versions of 5.1 m and 5.7 m, and 5.1 m is standard for the tractor units.

The engine fitted is the DAF DKA 11.6-litre 230 bhp naturally aspirated unit, with the DRS 320 bhp turbocharged and intercooled unit becoming available in 1981. The gearbox

is the ZF S-160 eight-speed unit with splitter.

The robust cab on the N-series is purpose-built for operation in hot climates and is well insulated and ventilated. It is made of steel with a plastics bonnet. The steel part is imported from Magirus Deutz of Ulm, in West Germany, but

This N 2800-series 6 × 4 tipper has a very robust construction to cope with the variety of difficult road and off-road conditions likely to be encountered in service.

the bonnet is imported from Norcem of Norway, the whole being assembled by DAF in Eindhoven.

The rear bogie is a Steyr double-drive unit rated at 26 tonnes and the front axle is a DAF 142, 6.5-tonne unit. Hot-weather features include a dust extractor and an air drier in the brake circuit, which automatically clears the system at regular intervals, an alternator with an air filter attached to extract dust, and an engine air-filter system consisting of a cyclinic unit in a vertical stack behind the cab with a second-stage filter element.

Estimated total market for the N series is 250 units in 1981, 500 in 1982 and 600 in 1983. On the 2100 and 2300 export series an annual production of 1,000 units is anticipated.

Export models of the DAF 2100 and 2300 series have also been introduced with countries in the Middle East and Africa especially in mind. The F 200 cab is fitted on both models.

The N 2800 series, shown here as an artic tractor unit, is designed specifically for the Middle Eastern and African markets.

Fitment of Trilex wheels is one external feature on this FA 2305 DHU export model which distinguishes it from a normal 2300-series design. Like the N 2800 series, it is designed specifically for Middle Eastern and African markets.

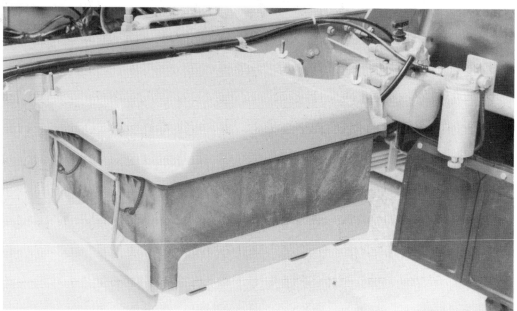

Well-sealed batteries on sturdy mountings are one of the detail features of the 2100/2300 series.

The designations 2100 and 2300 indicate that these versions have much in common with the similarly designated vehicles for Western European markets, the same main components being used. The engine, gearbox, axles and cab have, however, been fully adapted to the operating conditions in the territories mentioned, and will be available in 4 × 2, 6 × 2 and 6 × 4 configurations.

On three-axle chassis, the side-members are reinforced at the places subjected to the greatest stresses. On two-axle chassis in the 2300 series, the top and bottom flanges of the

The two-stage engine air-filter is particularly apparent in this photograph of the export version of the DAF 2100/2300 series.

Added strength is afforded in the F 2100/2300 export chassis by this method of attaching the cross-members to the chassis side-members.

side-members are provided with full-length reinforcements.

Chassis components have been positioned in such a way as to give good ground clearance and air reservoirs, fuel tanks and batteries are attached with very strong supports. The wheel housings are designed so as to permit the fitment of 20-in disc wheels or 24-in Trilex wheels, with the appropriate tyres.

Two engines are available for both models, the 163 bhp (120 kW) DH 825 and the 230 bhp (169 kW) DHU 825. A double-filtering air cleaner is designed to give the engine maximum protection against dust and sand. Transverse water-cooling and a fan and radiator of suitable dimensions for tropical conditions ensure that proper temperature control is maintained. Furthermore, the oil temperature is kept within reasonable limits by a large oil/water exchanger.

The DH and DHU engines are coupled to the ZF AK 6-65 and AK 6-80 gearbox, respectively, via a single-dry-plate clutch. There is the option of a splitter for the 2100 series,

doubling the number of speeds to 12; this splitter is standard on the 2300 series. Vehicles in the 2300 series can also be specified with the ZF 5K 90 GP gearbox, which has nine speeds, first gear being an extra-low crawler gear.

The 2100 series uses the DAF 2255 rear axle, combined with a trailing axle in the case of the FAS 2105. The 4 × 2 models in the 2300 series are fitted with the 2699 axle, which features hub reduction and incorporates a mechanical differential lock. The 2255 T tandem-axle unit is used for the 6 × 4 chassis in the 2300 series. It is equipped with an inter-axle differential.

Good engine access is provided on the N 2800 series by the plastics hood of the bonnet, which tilts forward.

The robust tandem axle of the N 2800 series showing the hub-reduction axles.

Although the cab interior of the N 2800 series is essentially functional, it offers an excellent standard of driver comfort and all-round vision is good.

Cab access on the N 2800 series is by two non-slip steps using grab handles just inside the doorway.

Chapter 7

DAF in the UK market

In 1980, DAF's biggest market for trucks outside the Netherlands was Britain; the Dutch company sold 2,300 vehicles there in 1979 and ranked as the No. 2 heavy-vehicle importer.

DAF heavy vehicles first appeared on the British market in 1966, but neither the British manufacturers, competitors nor leading operators took the Dutch company particularly seriously. Certainly there were very few people in the industry who would have predicted correctly DAF's position in the UK marketplace in 1980.

However, in 1966 they were right to discount the DAF incursion, because it was not a great success. It seems now that there was very little real planning behind the move. The first batch of DAFs arrived in Britain in August that year. The models introduced were from the company's 1800 and 1900 range; four-wheeled chassis built for both solo rigid duties at 16 tonnes gross vehicle weight and for articulated-vehicle operation at up to 28 tonnes gcw.

Initially, two British distributors were appointed — in the north, Ackworth Engineering Company Ltd, of Ackworth, near Pontefract, Yorkshire, and in the south, Chipping Sodbury Motor Company Ltd.

It was a commercial vehicle sellers' market in Britain at that time; the domestic manufacturers couldn't turn out trucks fast enough, so in a sense DAF were not wasting their time. They were bound to sell some.

In the event, the T 1800 DS tractor unit, in particular, proved quite popular. This was powered by the DS 575 diesel engine, rated at 150 bhp net at 2,400 rpm, and delivering 354 lb ft of torque at 1,700 rpm. The price in Britain, which today seems laughable though it was not unduly competitive then, was £3,750 complete in chassis-cab form.

The variations in models offered were quite extensive, even though not as great as those in the Netherlands. This was a mistake, but it generated a lesson so that it was not repeated when DAF remounted its attack on the UK market four years later.

For example, four wheelbase variants were offered for tipper and haulage applications under the general 1900 designation, and not all of them were suited to the British market. For instance, the shortest (11 ft 10 in wheelbase) chassis was restricted by the British Construction and Use Regulations to 15 tons gross. The rigid 1900s ranged in price from £3,800 to £3,870, according to wheelbase.

The bored-out version of the 575 engine, with a capacity of 6.17 litres, which had been introduced at the 1965 Amsterdam Show, was fitted in these vehicles to give them a power output of 126 bhp at 2,600 rpm and a maximum torque of 282 lb ft at 1,400 rpm, and all vehicles had a ZF six-speed gearbox and either a 5.72:1 or 6.33:1 hypoid-bevel back axle.

Although the cab fitted on these vehicles looked a bit dated, even to British operators, who were then not used to any great degree of cab sophistication, it was — to their surprise — very well finished and comfortable. Over 100 of

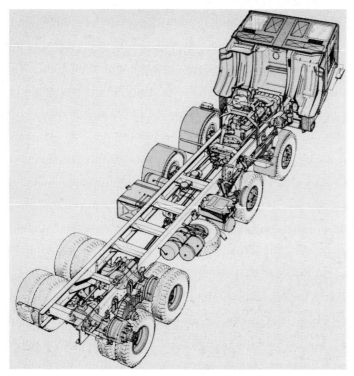

Designed in the UK, the DAF FAD 2205 DU 8 × 4 chassis, illustrated here with all-steel DAF 218 cab fully tilted.

these vehicles were imported into Britain from mid-1966 onwards.

Writing in the Earls Court Commercial Motor Show edition of *Commercial Vehicles* in October 1966, I reported that about 25 DAF tractor units had been sold at that point in Britain, mainly to relatively large-scale operators, who had workshops of their own with skilled personnel. Fairly extensive operational experience had been gained as a result, despite the absence of a dealer network and service organization. I then went on to report, 'DAF expects to build up such a network in Britain in due course, but admits that to do the job properly requires not only capital, but a good deal

of time'. This explains fairly explicitly why DAF's UK venture at this time did not meet with any great success. Distributor and spare-parts provision arrangements were not adequate.

What the incursion did do was provide the company with invaluable experience of the British market, bringing home to the Dutch management what was needed in the future. Lessons were learned which enabled DAF to adopt the correct formula for success when the management decided to renew the assault.

This second assault was mounted in 1970, when it was decided to set up a commercial vehicle division of DAF Motors, which was operating at that time from Feltham. The only commercial vehicle involvement then was with the DAF 7-cwt Variomatic delivery van. This was a London Commercial Motor Show year, and DAF was there for the first time, exhibiting three tractor units, a 2000, a 2200 and a 2600. The following year a test market programme was

The 24-tonnes gross FAT 2305 DHRE six-wheeled tipper made its first appearance in the UK in April, 1978. Features included the DAF DHRE 825 diesel engine, rated at 209 bhp at 2,400 rpm, and a ZF AK 6-80 six-speed constant-mesh gearbox. The chassis was also suitable for concrete-mixer use.

R.F. Interport Movements Ltd, of Leigh, Lancashire, was one of the first companies to buy the DAF FT 2800-based Supercontinental for its Middle East service.

undertaken, but the first DAF trucks did not start coming into the UK until late-1971.

It became clear in 1972 that DAF car and truck interests were unhappy bedfellows in the UK, and so, early in 1973, the car and truck operations in the UK were separated. DAF Trucks (GB) Ltd was formed with Mr David Mansell as its newly appointed managing director.

Within weeks, the new truck company moved to new premises comprising 35,000 ft² of warehouse and office space on the Thames Industrial Estate at Marlow. The new board tackled two matters straight away. The first was to select the range to be marketed, and it was decided that the UK company should concentrate on the top end of the premium-quality market — from 16 tonnes gvw up to the maximum permitted weights. The second point was parts-and-service backup. It was seen that this was an area in which DAF had been deficient in its earlier escapade in Britain, so it was vital

to provide proper facilities for the 21 main dealers being established.

The need to simplify servicing and parts stocking for these main dealers was recognized as a first principle, with the result that the vehicles imported into the UK were selected such that a minimum of different parts was required. At the time, DAF pointed out that while five sizes of engine were produced at Eindhoven, the 8.25 and 11.6-litre models took care of 95 per cent of DAF's UK requirements. Moreover, since the F 2800 models had the 11.6-litre engine and the cab had much in common with that of the F 2200 range, the introduction of the then new FT 2800 did not affect this policy.

To generate a high-quality DAF after-sales service, as an intermediate measure mechanics from each main dealer were sent on courses to the factory at Eindhoven to familiarize themselves with DAF vehicles and their components and plans were put in hand to establish a service training school at Marlow. This became operational early in 1974.

A DAF FAD 2205 DU 30-tonnes capacity 8 × 4 tipper of the type specially developed for the British market. Powered by an 8.25-litre turbocharged diesel engine, rated at 216 bhp and coupled to a 13-speed constant-mesh gearbox, the vehicle featured DAF's own two-spring tandem-axle bogie.

Just nine DAF vehicles were imported into Britain in 1971, and one of these was still in operation in 1980. This was the first, an FT 2000 sold by Charfield Commercial Sales to C. W. Vick, of Bristol; it had over 600,000 miles on the clock without a major fault developing when DAF bought it back as an historical memento in 1980.

When Mr Mansell arrived at Marlow he recruited his own management team and gave priority to the establishment of a good dealer network and parts facilities. Such was the effort put into this that, by October 1973, the network had been built with the planned 21 main dealers covering England, Wales, Scotland and Northern Ireland.

There was no Commercial Motor Show at Earls Court in 1973, but there was a Scottish Motor Show in Glasgow, and here DAF unveiled a model which was to be the main platform for its success in the UK. This was the FT 2800 tractor unit, a truly significant model in Britain, for by 1979 it had captured 54 per cent of the total tractor-unit market in its weight category.

Speaking at a pre-Scottish Show press gathering at the end

The constant-mesh gearbox on the FA 2105 DH was replaced in 1980 by the fully synchromesh ZF S 6-65 box with GV 80 splitter. Further modifications included the optimization of the drive line with an alternative rear-axle ratio option of 6.33:1.

DAF Trucks (Scotland) opened its purpose-built Grangemouth premises in 1978. They comprise an 8,000 ft² drive-through workshop, a 3,500 ft² parts area and a modern office block to accommodate sales, service, parts and accounts administration.

This unusual but impressive DAF FTT 2805 DKS recovery vehicle was exhibited in the livery of the Ben Cooper Group at the annual conference of the Association of Vehicle Recovery Operations at Chateau Impney, Droitwich, in 1980.

This attractive tanker outfit, operated by John Forman Ltd, of Hull, has a DAF FT 2300 DHU 36-ton, 4 × 2 tractor, powered by the 8.25-litre turbocharged diesel engine. Rated at 230 bhp, it is coupled to a ZF AK 5 K-91 GP nine-speed constant-mesh gearbox. The vehicle was one of the exhibits at the 1979 Scottish Motor Show.

of October 1973, Dave Mansell reviewed the three main targets for the year which he had set the company on January 1 when DAF Trucks (GB) Ltd had been formed.

These were: To establish a suitable base and build up a competent team of people; appoint at least 20 main dealers throughout the UK; and sell and deliver 500 trucks to customers. As indicated, the first two goals had already been achieved. As for the third target, some 375 vehicles had already been shipped to customers through DAF's dealer network, and Mr Mansell reported that the order book was extremely healthy. 'Next year', said Mr Mansell, 'DAF plans to double its UK business.' It did!

The right-hand-drive version of the FT 2800 DKTD tractor on show in Glasgow was not the only innovation from DAF

Phil Ives, who was appointed managing director of DAF Trucks (GB) Ltd in 1978.

Ltd, of Rutherglen, near Glasgow.

Handing the vehicle over to the operator, DAF (GB)'s sales manager said: 'Our growth has been rapid but stable, and we aim to maintain it. DAF's UK target for 1975 is 1,500 vehicles, and 2,000 vehicles by 1976. Above all we shall be concentrating on the quality market, among operators with a farsighted approach to business who demand first-class parts-and-service back-up and can appreciate the cost-saving benefits of our products.' DAF was on the march.

1974 was a Commercial Motor Show year at London's Earls Court, and four models, one completely new and two

David Mansell, the first managing director of DAF Trucks (GB) Ltd. He is now a member of the Board of Management of DAF Trucks in Eindhoven, with responsibility for worldwide sales and marketing.

at the 1973 Scottish Show. There was also an FA 2200 DU 4 × 2, designed for both solo and drawbar work, with a matching DAF drawbar trailer. This was the first all-DAF truck-and-trailer unit brought into Britain — quite a novelty.

In a market which was starting at that time to get tough, DAF, in July 1974, sold its 1,000th vehicle in Britain — a 36-tonne FT 2200 DU tractor unit for the haulage fleet of Transport Development Group subsidiary J. & R. Wright

A DAF FA 1600 DT cab and chassis fitted with a 23 ft body constructed from 17 mm thick Glasonit by Frank Guy, of Clay Cross, Derbyshire, for express parcels carrier Plackett's Transport of Stapleford, Nottingham.

more on show for the first time, formed the DAF line-up. The centrepiece was the FAD 2205 DU eight-wheeler and a right-hand-drive example of the most powerful DAF on offer — the 307 bhp charge-cooled DKS tractor unit, rated at 56 tonnes for Continental road operation and the first DAF with a charge-cooled engine to be seen in Britain.

Until this point, DAF had not offered an eight-wheeler in the UK, and the FAD 2205 DU was in fact a completely new 8 × 4 tipper designed specifically for the UK market. Here was a landmark for DAF — its first design purpose-built for British requirements and, more significantly, perhaps, the DAF (GB) staff had played quite a significant role in its design and development. This vehicle was intended primarily for maximum-weight tipper operation. At a plated weight of 30 tonnes and with a nominal unladen weight of eight tonnes, it offered a body and payload allowance of 22 tonnes — 20

per cent more than a six-wheeler and approaching the maximum possible with an articulated vehicle under UK legislation. It was fitted with a 216 bhp turbocharged DAF six-cylinder engine, DAF double-drive bogie with standard lockable-third differential and 13-speed Fuller constant-mesh RTO 613 gearbox with crawler and overdrive top. Tipper bodies up to 23 ft long could be accommodated on the flat-topped channel-section chassis, which was reinforced with a full-length frame liner. Standard equipment included power steering and a DAF 218 tilt cab.

DAF continued its aggressive sales activities in Britain in 1974, Mr Mansell announcing at the end of August that year that the plan was to expand DAF's UK sales in the next two years by 80 per cent.

The UK, said Mr Mansell, was a key part of the European market for DAF. It also happened to be the largest 10-tonne-

One of the first of the FT 2200 series to arrive in the UK was this unit destined to haul bulk tipper trailers for J. & R. Wright, of Liverpool.

plus market in Europe (55,000 vehicles a year) and, regardless of whether DAF sold trucks in Britain, a company had to be established in the UK to provide service for DAF's European customers.

He gave a run-down on progress to that date and it is worth, several years on, recalling what he said, for it reflects the whole sales-and-marketing philosophy of DAF at that time in Britain.

He commented: 'Our truck range has been limited to 13 models in the interest of rationalization and interchangeability of parts and components. We now have 22 main dealers, strategically located throughout the country. The next phase of our development will be the appointment of sub-dealers specializing in service and parts. Training in all its aspects will remain high on the list of priorities. Our own training school at Marlow has been in operation since the beginning of the year.

'In summary, DAF is all set to capture a fair slice of the UK market. Regardless of the current economic uncertainties now facing the country, we believe the demand for quality vehicles at the top-end of the range will grow. Fleet operators are professional people with an awareness of what quality means in terms of total operating costs — low fuel and maintenance costs, coupled with reliability, are the yardsticks of today. The driver of today is also very discerning and a more professional individual, and must be amply catered for. DAF are ready and geared to these needs.'

Following their debut at the Earls Court Commercial Motor Show of 1974, two pre-production examples of the DAF FAD 2205 DU 8 × 4 tippers were exhibited at the 1975 Road Haulage Association Tipper Show. They had been undergoing intensive field trials with British operators. The duties included a month on sand-and-gravel haulage in the Peak District with John Owen (Aggregates) Ltd, of Sheffield, and a month on preparation work on the Thames Barrier scheme carrying heavy clay for C. M. Ellerby and Sons, of Dartford. Then came heavy-haulage work for English China Clays, based on Plympton, Devon. This particular tipper then went to work for Springbank Sand and Gravel, in Stirlingshire. Coal haulage was the work of the second vehicle, and it covered two extremes of this business — general work in hilly country for the Golightly Group, of Durham, as well as maximum-payload operation in Nottinghamshire with K and M Haulage Ltd, of Hucknall. Both vehicles were fitted with Wilcox aluminium bodies. The FAD 2205 DU, plated at 30 tonnes gvw, offered a body/payload allowance of 22 tonnes.

DAF also announced a raised air-intake of special design to avoid contamination of the oil-bath air-cleaner in bad on-site conditions. This came about as a bonus from the field-testing of the FAD 2205s. As well as being located 7 ft above ground level, the new unit was designed to induce swirl and turbulence, ensuring good moisture separation; moisture recovered from the airstream was collected in a removable, durable, semi-transparent container.

The eight-wheeler went into production shortly after the tipper show. The first production model was delivered to owner-driver Michael Hobson, of Buckley, Clwyd. With a steel-floored tipper body the vehicle had a payload of 20.2 tonnes within a maximum gross vehicle weight of 30 tonnes. This particular vehicle had two unusual features. An Edbro 6LNC tipping gear was fitted low down behind the cab to give

DAF's 2000 series quickly established itself in distribution work. This 1978-registered vehicle was bought for the national distribution of pallet loads of ice-cream to frozen food centres. It is powered by DAF's 8.25-litre diesel, producing 156 bhp, matched with a ZF AK six-speed constant-mesh gearbox and two-speed splitter.

DAF didn't just import trucks into the UK; it looked for something extra, and this photograph shows one of the measures taken in 1975. Due to the wide variations encountered by DAF truck dealers when fitting fifth wheels to tractor units, DAF made available a wheel subframe plus lead-on ramps. To complete the tractor package, wing stays, wings and an alloy catwalk were also offered.

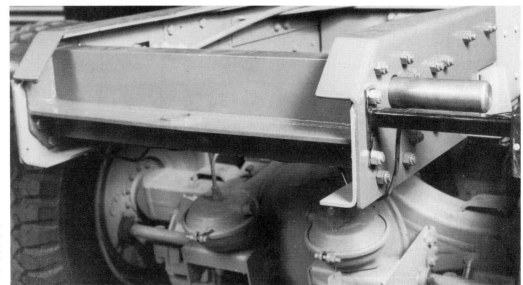

The care taken by DAF to ensure that vehicles are right for the job they have to do is reflected in this 1975 photograph. In order that tipper bodies were fitted in a manner approved by DAF, a mandatory option was fitted to eight-wheeled tipper chassis, during the pre-delivery check at DAF's main workshops, comprising a rear hinge pin fitted through a special cross-member and chassis-reinforcing flitches.

This FT 2800, fitted with a box van semi-trailer and engaged on transcontinental haulage duties, was one of a wide diversity of vehicles being offered by DAF in the UK by 1974.

an overall height of only 2.75 metres for maximum clearance when operating under low hoppers, and it had a sleeper cab to overcome the problem of finding good accommodation at short notice.

1975 was a poor year for the truck market in the UK, but at the end of it DAF had taken the No. 2 importer spot in both the 28-tonnes-plus tractor market and the heavy, two-axle, three-axle and tractor market combined with a penetration of 6.6 per cent of the total heavy tractor market and 15.3 per cent of the imported heavy tractor market.

The mid-1970s were the boom years for international haulage to the Middle East, and it was again on the British

company's initiative that DAF created the Supercontinental, following requests by a large number of transport operators. This was a special version of the F 2800 series, and it was designed to meet the extremely severe conditions which are still encountered on international transport routes, and in particular on those to the Middle East.

The cab of the Supercontinental was based on the standard sleeper cab, but it had additional equipment, such as a cooker, a refrigerator, a sink unit, air-conditioning and a space heater. The purpose of the additional equipment was to make the driver completely self-supporting on his journeys to his distant destinations and to give him extremely comfortable surroundings.

The technical specification of the vehicle was also modified to meet the greatly fluctuating climatic conditions, particular attention being given to engine-cooling. The cooling-system capacity of the 320 bhp (DIN) engine was increased to cope with extremely high ambient temperatures, a cyclone-type filter being fitted for operation in abnormally dusty conditions and a flame starter provided to get the engine going at sub-zero temperatures.

The self-locking differential, a feature of the F 2800 DKS model, was an obvious help on bad road surfaces. Twin foglamps and two spotlights incorporated in a specially designed bumper provided something extra in all-round vision and, like the four standard headlights, they were protected by lamp guards. The radiator also had a guard to protect it, and the windscreen was of laminated glass, making this one of the first trucks to be so fitted. There was also an external sun visor extending over the full width of the cab and deflectors attached on either side of the cab at the front kept the side windows free of excessive dirt on muddy stretches.

It was stressed that this new F 2800 version could be supplied to any market, but that it should not be regarded as a specific new model; rather, it was an example of the way in which DAF could meet the special requirements of a particular kind of transport using standard and special accessories.

1976 was 'Women's Year', so DAF Trucks (GB) thought the chance was ideal to turn the spotlight on the part played by British women in the world of road haulage. This was achieved through the 'Lady Lorry Driver of the Year Competition', in which lady drivers in possession of HGV licences could compete. This contest was staged at Hucknall, Nottinghamshire, on a closed-down section of an airfield, where there was plenty of room for the competition and peripheral activities.

Who won? It's history now. Attractive, blonde, 23-year-old Lesley Smith, a heavy-vehicle driver with Arden Wall Freezing and Cold Store Services, in Kirksandall (Doncaster), was judged the best of the finalists and, as a consequence, she gave up her job and joined DAF Trucks (GB) Ltd as a demonstration driver. She must like the job for at the time of

An interesting application for an FT 2200 six-wheeler fitted with concrete mixer bodywork and ancillary gear, and dating from 1973.

writing she is still with the organization.

Unfortunately, when the Sex Discrimination Act was introduced it was ruled that men could not be excluded from the competition — which rather lost the point of any 'Lady Lorry Driver' contest.

DAF by now was growing in prestige as well as in numbers in Britain, and it had become a question of what else could be done to secure the company's position. One of the measures taken was to introduce DAFaid, a 24-hour emergency telephone support scheme. Operated throughout the UK by DAF's main-dealer network, DAFaid was set up to provide emergency help and information at any time of the day or night throughout the year.

Under the scheme, any operator of a DAF truck automatically qualified for inclusion — at no extra cost to either the operator or the driver. A central telephone number was provided for a DAF driver to phone in an emergency. Contact ensured that help was quickly provided by the nearest

DAF Trucks dealer, whether roadside repairs, broken windscreens or information on security parks, hotels or parking restrictions, were involved. A spares service guaranteed delivery of a spare part to virtually anywhere within 24 hours of the dealer being notified.

This DAFaid scheme was linked with the DAF Trucks ITS (International Truck Service) scheme on the Continent. This scheme permits the British driver of a DAF vehicle stranded on the Continent to refer to his ITS booklet, supplied as part of the truck kit, to obtain the central ITS telephone number in Eindhoven, or the location and telephone number of his nearest DAF Trucks service centre.

In the event of repairs being necessary to the truck, the driver can get his vehicle repaired quickly without having to pay cash. This is achieved by means of a credit guarantee arrangement operating throughout the DAF Trucks service network. A telephone call to the dealer which supplied the DAF truck ensures that the appropriate credit guarantee is obtained and, on production of the driver's DAF service credit card, repairs on the truck will be carried out immediately.

When the second-generation DAF F 2800s, which had been launched at the 1980 Amsterdam Show, appeared on the UK market later in the year, a further service was announced. This was DAF Medicair, a scheme under which injured or sick drivers on international operation can be brought back home when medical care in the country concerned is not up to UK standards.

Utilizing the facilities of Jetdoctor International, DAF's ITS control centre in Eindhoven makes the necessary arrangements, and a particular feature of the scheme is that it is 'vehicle-linked', which means that it can be used regardless of which driver is using the relevant vehicle abroad.

All new purchasers of second-generation F 2800s have free-of-charge cover for the first 12 months, and after this the cover can be renewed annually for a nominal charge.

Cove's Transport used this FA 2200 DU rigid vehicle and trailer with high-sided containers for the movement of precision engineering goods in 1974.

Reflecting the general success of the 2800 series, this FT 2800 DKTD delivered in 1980 was one of a number of similar vehicles ordered by Greenwoods Transport Ltd, of Hoddesdon, Hertfordshire, following good experience with the first 2800-series vehicles it bought in 1976.

By 1977, DAF was geared to step up its assault on the British market and the Scottish Motor Show in that year was to provide the opportunity. There had been, and was still, a lot of work going on North of the Border. Scrutiny of the Scottish market had revealed that more than 10 per cent of UK heavy-truck sales were in Scotland. It was for this reason that, in 1975, DAF Trucks (GB) had decided to acquire its Scottish dealership and establish DAF Trucks (Scotland) Ltd, at Banknock, Stirlingshire. The facilities were inadequate for the operation envisaged by DAF, so plans were drawn-up to develop a custom-built truck complex on a 6½-acre site at Westmains Industrial Estate, Grangemouth, at a cost of approximately £½ million. This would include an 8,000 ft² drive-through workshop, a 3,500 ft² parts area, and a modern office block to accommodate sales, service, parts and accounts administration.

The first turf was cut in April 1977, and the complex was complete and functional by early-March 1978. During the construction period, in 1977, DAF Trucks (Scotland) sold 176 trucks from the Banknock facility, and in just over two years the company's turnover increased to £3.2m a year.

This was the scene in Scotland at the time of the 1977 Scottish Show, in Glasgow; construction of the new complex had yet to be completed, but the market opportunities in Scotland were clearly there. They were also present in the rest of Britain, so the unveiling of new models was not for Scotland alone.

Although on public view at a British motor show for the first time, the FT 2300 4 × 2 tractor unit, which formed one of the main exhibits in Glasgow, had been introduced at the beginning of 1977. This 36-tonne design was already proving popular throughout the country, for 26 per cent of DAF's sales were in this vehicle class.

Powered by DAF's 8.25-litre turbocharged, charge-cooled engine rated at 230 bhp and generating a torque of 571 lb ft, this vehicle was showing up very well on fuel tests, a leading journal getting an average of 7.88 mpg on road test at 32 tonnes gross weight.

Maximum economy was being looked for by operators at this time, and DAF's introduction of this vehicle proved popular. The same went for a second vehicle, which went on show for the first time in Britain at the 1977 Scottish Motor Show. This was the DAF F 2100 series, which was aimed specifically at the short-medium-haul operator requiring a vehicle in the 28-32-tonnes weight category. Using many of

the design features incorporated in the DAF F 2300 and F 2800 series, the tractor unit was powered by the DAF DHR 825, 8.25-litre turbocharged diesel, then newly developed and incorporating transverse cooling and an oil-cooler/heat-exchanger. Rated at 202 bhp, the DAF DHR 825 engine had a maximum torque output of 494 lb ft and was matched with a ZF AK 6-65 six-speed gearbox and GV 80 two-speed splitter box.

A third vehicle at this Scottish Show was a 51-tonne DKS version of DAF's F 2800 series. This was powered by DAF's biggest engine, the DAF DKS 1160 turbocharged, charge-cooled diesel, rated at 307 bhp and fitted with a 13-speed Fuller RTO 9513 constant-mesh gearbox with single-dry-

Operated by Tesco Stores Ltd, the UK's biggest multiple retailer, this is one of a number of DAF FT 2300 DHU 4 × 2 tractors to be used for long-distance trunking throughout the UK, transporting goods destined for the 'Home and Wear' departments in over 350 Tesco stores.

A 1976-registered DAF FTT 2805 DKS 6 × 4 56-ton gcw tractive unit being used with a special oscillating bolster on the fifth wheel to transport concrete beams weighing 30 tons and measuring 87 ft 6 in long. The bogie is equipped with powered rear steering.

plate, air-assisted, hydraulically operated clutch. An unusual point about this vehicle was that the DAF hub-reduction rear-axle assembly was fitted with a lockable differential, a feature which from this point on was available on all 4 × 2 and 6 × 2 models of the 2800 series.

So to the spring of 1978, when a major change occurred for DAF in Britain. Mr David Mansell, who had guided DAF to its success in the UK, was promoted to the main board of DAF Trucks at Eindhoven and put in charge there of the company's total marketing and sales activities. At Marlow, Mr Phil Ives, who had joined DAF as deputy managing director only a few months before, took over the reins as the new managing director.

Commenting on the changes, Mr Ives said at the time:

The FT 2300, which was launched into the UK market at the 1976 Commercial Vehicle Show, had recorded 1,500 registrations by the time of the 1979 Scottish Motor Show, such had been its popularity. This tanker example is carrying plastics pellets.

'DAF Trucks has really gone places in these five years; our order book is extremely high and we are making very positive roads into the heavy end of this very competitive truck market. I look forward to carrying on from the strong base established through five years of hard work by David Mansell and his team. These results are particularly significant when one considers that DAF Trucks are a totally independent organization manufacturing purely trucks and truck components.'

The news of Mr Ives' appointment broke during the 1978 Road Haulage Association Tipper Convention. There, DAF was showing its FAT 2305 DHRE 6 × 4 rigid tipper, which was making its first appearance in the UK and was seen with a Neville Ultralite body. Also in the picture was a premium FAD 2205 DU 8 × 4 rigid tipper fitted with the new Telehoist Monolite 15.3 cu m sand-and-gravel body and Telehoist tipping gear. Their presence at this show revealed the emphasis placed by DAF on this sector of the market. It reflected the company's growing success in rigid-vehicle sales as well as those of tractor units.

This drive to penetrate the UK tipper market continued in 1979 with new high-specification 2300 rigids of 6 × 4 and 8 × 4 configuration. An all-synchromesh gearbox was one of the features introduced, claimed to enhance the trucks' driver appeal. For lighter duties, the company offered the FA 2105DH, a 4 × 2 with a payload of about 10 tonnes.

Early in 1980, DAF stepped-up its efforts in the tipper-and-mixer sector with the introduction of the FTA 2305 DHRE 6 × 4 chassis with a 4.25 m wheelbase. A load of over 15 tonnes was possible on this 24-tonne gvw vehicle, which features the DAF DHRE 8.25-litre diesel engine, rated at 209 bhp at 2,400 rpm, coupled to a ZF AK 6-80 six-speed constant-mesh gearbox. This engine is a more powerful version of the DAF DHR 825 from which it was developed.

Specially designed chassis reinforcements and heavy-duty rear springs are incorporated on the new vehicle, without adding to the weight. The vehicle is equipped with 12—22.5 tyres on the front axle to give a rating of 6,500 kg (6 × 4 tonnes).

A useful point about it is that a body-installation kit is available, thus removing the need for bodybuilders to carry out chassis work. The kit comprises a tipping rear cross-member complete with tipping bar and front body guides. Where mixer specification is required, a full mounting kit is now available, having been developed through discussions with the UK's mixer manufacturers. This kit provides strategically positioned side plates to enable the mixer sub-frame to be simply placed on the chassis and welded into position. On the new chassis, front stabilizers are a standard fitment.

In September 1978, DAF held a press conference in London and Mr Ives said that uncertainty over Parliamentary elections in the UK, coupled with difficulties over the Government's pay policy, made 1979 market prospects for the heavy-vehicle market 'not encouraging'. Fortunately he was wrong, for the bad times did not come until 1980. DAF was still No. 2 heavy-vehicle importer in Britain and was enjoying its highest-ever level of truck sales. DAF sales were 24.5 per cent more than forecast.

DAF's main increase in sales came in the three and four-axled rigid-vehicle sectors. This was not to say that DAF tractor sales had fallen off, for a month later the company reported that, since its introduction on to the UK market in 1974, the DAF 2800 heavy-duty tractor unit had climbed steadily up the popularity scale, and the 2,000th example had been delivered. Although the lighter-weight 2300 tractor arrived in Britain some two years later, its sales had reached four figures, the 1,000th going into service in July 1979.

As it turned out, DAF had a good year in Britain in 1979, Mr Ives being able to report that in the market for vehicles over 14.5 tonnes, which had clocked up 36,000 sales and was up 30 per cent on the previous year, DAF's market share had risen by 22 per cent in 1979 compared with 1978.

Mr Ives thought 1980 would be tougher, not only because of the economic climate, but because the opposition had made forward strides. This time his views on the state of the market have unfortunately been proved absolutely right. Nevertheless, with such a strong and diversified product range, DAF Trucks would seem to be well-equipped to weather such storms as the turbulent 1980s may produce.